Gradatim

A progressive course in Unseen and
Comprehension Passages in O-level Latin

J G F Potter
Awarder and Chief Examiner in O-level
classics for the Oxford Delegacy of Local Examinations

Oxford University Press

Oxford University Press, Walton Street, Oxford OX2 6DP

OXFORD LONDON GLASGOW
NEW YORK TORONTO MELBOURNE AUCKLAND
KUALA LUMPUR SINGAPORE HONG KONG TOKYO
DELHI BOMBAY CALCUTTA MADRAS KARACHI
NAIROBI DAR ES SALAAM CAPE TOWN

and associated companies in
BERUIT BERLIN IBADAN MEXICO CITY NICOSIA

Oxford is a trade mark of Oxford University Press

ISBN 0 19 8317794

© Oxford University Press 1978

First printed 1978
Reprinted 1979, 1981, 1984

Printed in Great Britain by
J. W. Arrowsmith Ltd., Bristol.

Introduction

All the Unseens in this book, and ten of the fifteen
Comprehension Passages, were set by me for the O-level
examination of the Oxford Delegacy of Local Examinations. I
wish to express my gratitude to the Oxford Delegacy for
permission to reprint these Unseens and Comprehension
Passages, and I express particular thanks to Mr. J.R. Cummings,
who, as Secretary of the Delegacy at the time, gave me his
personal approval.

The Unseens in this book have been arranged to provide a
progressive course. To this end, the first seventeen Unseens have
been adapted, in pairs, so that the main Latin constructions are
introduced progressively. For example, the first two Unseens are
substantially as they appeared when set at O Level, but all the
main constructions, except for Accusative and Infinitive, have
been eliminated. In the second pair of Unseens, Purpose Clauses
are introduced – and of course further practice with the Accusative
and Infinitive construction, which has just been covered, can now
be incorporated. The third pair introduce Indirect Commands;
and this progressive method is followed through, until, by
Unseen no. 17, all the main constructions have been covered. The
rest of the Unseens are printed exactly as they appeared when they
were set in the O-Level examination.

Each construction is introduced by a brief explanation, in
which the emphasis is on the particular difficulties which the
construction may cause for translators from Latin to English.

The obvious advantage of this progressive method is that, by
tackling these Unseens in the order in which they are given,
candidates can be introduced to, or can revise, the main
constructions one at a time, instead of being discouraged by a
mixed bag of constructions, some of which, at the beginning of
their O-Level year, they cannot be expected to handle. The first

eighteen Unseens, i.e., those in which constructions are progressively introduced, have been so arranged that there is a pair of Unseens for each construction. This will enable teachers, if they so wish, to let their pupils work the first Unseen of each pair as introduction and the second of each pair as revision. With this possibility in mind, I have given a fair amount of advice about the first Unseen in each pair and very little advice about the second.

Besides explanations of constructions, sections are also included on how to tackle Unseens and Comprehension Passages. All this explanatory matter is addressed to the candidates themselves. This is simply because, having seen the game from both sides of the fence, as teacher and as examiner, I am in a position to give them advice which will enable them to avoid traps into which, over many years, I have seen so many candidates fall quite unnecessarily.

Finally, I wish to acknowledge help received. First, I would like to record my gratitude to Mr. Colin Dexter, Senior Assistant Secretary at the Oxford Delegacy, who not only corrected the proofs of this book but also gave me invaluable aid by pertinent criticisms of its subject-matter and by many helpful suggestions for its improvement. Second, I would like to pay particular tribute to Mr. S.A. Handford. It was under Mr. Handford's supervision that I worked, from 1935, as examiner and (later) as paper-setter, until I succeeded him, ten years ago, as Awarder and Chief Examiner in O-Level Classics for the Oxford Delegacy. Apart from enjoying the privilege of this association with a man who is unrivalled as a Latinist in this country at present, I learned most of what I know about examining and paper-setting from Mr. Handford.

Contents

How to tackle an Unseen

Before you look at the Latin of an Unseen, read its English title carefully. The title may give you nothing more than a rough summary of what the Unseen is about. On the other hand, it may give you, in various ways, information which is extremely helpful. a) If the Unseen contains any unusual proper names, the title will explain them for you. For example, one of the Unseens in this book begins with the word **Austoriani**. Is it a proper name? The capital 'A' is no help, since the first word in any Unseen must begin with a capital letter. It could, therefore, be **austoriani** – some word which you don't happen to have met. Even if you decide that it is a proper name, you have still got a problem: what kind of proper name? (A place-name? A man's name? A people?) In fact, there is no problem of any kind, because the title of this Unseen is: 'An African tribe, the Austoriani, pillage the Lepcitani, who appeal to the Romans for help.' Obviously the word **Lepcitani** must also occur in this Unseen, though not necessarily in the nominative case. It does occur – in the first sentence and in the genitive plural form **Lepcitanorum** = 'of the Lepcitani'. Without the help of the title, there is not the smallest doubt that a number of candidates would have contrived to take the word as the accusative singular of a proper name **Lepcitanorus**. (It must be recorded that, in spite of the title, which they clearly hadn't bothered to read, a few candidates did take the word as an accusative singular when this Unseen was worked in the O-Level examination a few years ago.) b) The title will sometimes give you the meaning of an unusual word or phrase. In one of the Unseens in this book, you will find the phrase **utribus stramento refertis**. You are very unlikely to know the meaning of any of these words. The phrase means '(with) skins stuffed with straw' – words which no examiner in his senses could expect O-Level candidates to have met. But examiners *do* expect O-Level candidates to read the title, which is: 'Arriving at the river Oxus, Alexander transports his

1

men with the aid of skins stuffed with straw.' c) The title, without giving you the meaning of a word directly, may help you to work out the meaning of it. Take, as an example, the phrase **milites siti gravi oppressi sunt**. There is not much difficulty with subject and verb: 'the soldiers were overwhelmed/oppressed'. But **siti** is not a particularly common word, and you may not know it. It appears to be a noun, since the adjective **gravi** (which you should know) cannot agree with **milites** and must therefore agree with **siti**. **Siti gravi** could be dative or ablative singular (nothing else is possible). Passive verbs are frequently followed by an ablative, and, if this is so here, the meaning is 'the soldiers were overwhelmed by grave/serious (——)'. The title of the Unseen from which the phrase has been taken is: 'Thirsty soldiers die from drinking too much water.' The first two words, 'thirsty soldiers', should tell you that 'thirst' is the word to fill the gap. d) Very occasionally, when a Latin word occurs which can have two or more meanings, the title may help you to arrive at the one which the context requires. You will find a good example of this in the first Unseen in this book. In the second line of this Unseen, Labienus is described as having been **legatus Caesaris**. In Appendix A, you will find the two meanings of **legatus** listed thus: 'ambassador', 'general' (the latter serving under a commander-in-chief who will be called **imperator**). Is Labienus Caesar's ambassador or his general? The title reads: 'Labienus, who had served under Caesar . . .'. 'General' is therefore right, and 'ambassador' – in this context – will have to be marked wrong.

Having read the title carefully, turn to the Unseen itself. Difficulties of translation come under two main headings: a) Vocabulary, i.e., the meanings of the words; b) Syntax, i.e., how the words are strung together. Since you have obviously got to begin with the words, it is logical to think about Vocabulary first. All the same, you cannot be warned too early that, at O Level, far more marks are lost by failure to see how the words are strung together than by ignorance of the words themselves. Ignorance of one word will, *in itself*, lose you just one mark; and there is no need to get in a panic if, when you read through an Unseen for the first time, you find that there are as many as half a dozen words that you don't know. As you will shortly be shown, there are ways of working out their meanings (apart from the help, already illustrated, which the title may give). If these ways fail (as of course they may), your ignorance of six words will still only cost you six marks (out of a total of 40 or thereabouts) *provided that you can see, from the case-endings, verb-endings etc., how the words are strung together*. An example already quoted will illustrate this: **milites siti gravi oppressi sunt**. If you are careless enough to ignore the title but sensible enough to see how the words are strung together, you will write: 'the soldiers were overwhelmed by serious (———)'. You will lose only one mark. On the other hand, if your translation is 'the soldiers seriously overwhelmed the site', you will lose the lot, i.e., whatever the allocation of marks may have been for the whole phrase. Renderings as bad as this *are* produced by O–Level candidates; and the section on syntax aims to prevent them. But first there is quite a bit to be said about Vocabulary.

O–Level Unseens do not demand a wide vocabulary; and you should be able to acquire one which is wide enough from your reading of Latin authors and from grammar books (where the lists of principal parts of verbs are particularly important). If any really unusual word does occur, its meaning will be given to you. Always look below the Unseen itself to see whether any glossary of such words is provided. This may seem quite unnecessary advice, but any G.C.E. examiner would tell you that there are always candidates who throw away marks by ignoring the glossary. If the Unseen contains words which you haven't met, you may still be able to work out their meaning.

First, English derivatives are often a considerable help. In the first Unseen in this book, the following words occur: **pestilentia**, **autumni**, **consumpsit**, **resistere**, **victorem**. (I have set them out here in the forms in which they occur in the Unseen.) They mean: 'pestilence', 'autumn', 'consume', 'resist', 'victor'. These are easy examples; but most Unseens contain words the meaning of which an English derivative will either give you directly or help you to obtain. Thus, the second Unseen in this book contains the words **discordia**, **occasionem**, **trepidatio**, **creatum esse**, **creaverunt**, **seditione**, all of which have English derivatives which will help you to get their meaning. I say 'help', because, in the context, you will find that, for **discordia**, 'disagreement' is a better translation than 'discord', and that, for **occasionem**, 'opportunity' is better than 'occasion', though **trepidatio** and **seditione** can perfectly well be translated as 'trepidation' and 'sedition'. The two words **creatum esse** and

3

creaverunt are both parts of the same verb **creo**. Something which will be very useful to you is revealed here: English derivatives from Latin verbs are usually formed from what, in the jargon of grammar books, is called the supine-stem of the verb. The principal parts of this verb are: **creo, -are, creavi, creatum**. The English word 'create' is derived from **creatum**, i.e., from the supine-stem. From the form **creaverunt** you would be unlikely to get the meaning 'create'. You will certainly get it from **creatum esse** – a part of the verb which is formed from the supine-stem. A couple of other examples may help to reinforce this point:

    misceo, -ere, miscui, <u>mixtum</u> = mix
    consulo, -ere, consului, <u>consultum</u> = consult

Sometimes the meaning of a Latin *verb* can be obtained by way of an English *noun* derived from the supine-stem. E.g.,

    frango, -ere, fregi, <u>fractum</u>   English noun: 'fracture'.
                             Latin verb means 'break'.
    iungo, -ere, iunxi, <u>iunctum</u>   English noun: 'junction'.
                             Latin verb means 'join'.

Of course your ability to use derivatives must depend on the extent of your English vocabulary. The second Unseen in this book contains the word **plebem**. You could get its meaning from the English adjective 'plebeian' – not a common English word, and knowledge of it implies a fairly wide English vocabulary. Although, as it happens, there is no English noun derived from the Latin noun **plebs**, there is no shortage of English nouns, as well as adjectives, derived from Latin nouns. Just as English words derived from Latin verbs usually come from the supine-stem, so English words derived from Latin nouns usually come from the noun-stem, which the nominative singular often conceals but which the genitive singular always reveals. E.g.,

    caput, capitis: 'head', 'capital'
    origo, originis: 'origin'
    iter, itineris: 'journey', 'itinerary'
    os, oris: 'mouth'; English adjective; 'oral'
    vulnus, vulneris: 'wound'; English adjective; 'vulnerable'

There are a couple of snags regarding the use of English derivatives.

The first is that, even with some well-known English words, the connection between the English derivative and its Latin original is not obvious. Almost all O-Level candidates would know the English word 'incinerator'. But could they deduce from it the meaning of the Latin word **cinis, cineris**? (It means 'ash', because 'incinerator' by derivation means 'maker of ashes'.) Most O-Level candidates would know the English word 'pulverize'. But not very many could deduce from it the meaning of **pulvis, pulveris**. (It means 'dust', because the literal meaning of 'pulverize' is 'reduce to dust'.) The second (and much more serious) snag is that some English derivatives come from Latin words which changed their meaning during the long history of the Latin language. A simple (and very common) example will make this clear. The English verb 'instruct' is derived from **instruo, -ere, instruxi, instructum**. But in the sort of Latin you meet (Latin of the Classical Period) **instruo** very seldom means 'instruct'. The word only acquired this as its usual meaning in the colloquial Latin of a much later period. (It is from such Latin that English derivatives largely come.) You will find **instruo** (in the form **instruxisset**) in the first Unseen in this book; and its meaning – in any Latin that you are likely to see at O Level – is given in Appendix A. Similarly, in any Latin you are likely to see at O Level, **contendere** very seldom means 'contend', and **committere** – in the common phrase **committere proelium** – does not mean 'commit'. You will find both words, with the meanings which you will require, in Appendix A. One further point about derivatives: English often derives, not from the simple Latin verb, but from the verb compounded with a prefix; and you will come across some examples in which the prefix makes the derivation difficult to spot. For instance, candidates sometimes do not know the meaning of **maneo**. In later Latin it was commonly used with the prefix **re-, remaneo**. It would be easily recognisable in this form, but of course you will meet the word without the prefix. Similarly, although **cernere** means 'discern', the English word is derived from the form **discernere**. **Vertere** means 'turn' – and there is an English word 'vert', but it is so rarely used that few people would know it. Nevertheless, there are a number of words derived from **vertere** compounded with a prefix, e.g., 'revert', 'convert', 'subvert', as well as nouns such as 'conversion', 'inversion' etc., which are derived from the supine-stem of **verto, -ere, verti, versum**.

You have a chance of further help from derivatives if you are learning a modern language based directly (as English is not) on Latin, e.g., French, Italian, Spanish. Of these languages, Italian is the closest to Latin, but few O-Level candidates study Italian. On the other hand, many candidates take French, and, if you are one of them, remember that French derivatives can be a help. You will not get the meaning of **pons, pontis** from the English word 'bridge', but you will get it at once if you know the French word **pont** (Italian: **ponte**). Here are other examples. **Lingua** = 'tongue' – French **langue**; Italian **lingua**. **Panis** = 'bread' – French **pain**; Italian **pane**. If you meet the Latin word **fluvius** (as you may, at O Level, though of course **flumen** is much commoner) you can get the meaning of it provided that you know that the French word for 'river' is **fleuve**. (Italian would be no help here, as it uses **fiume** derived from **flumen**.) If, therefore, you find in front of you an unfamiliar word which has no obvious English derivative, it is worth your while to see whether you can think of a word like it in any Latin-based language that you happen to be studying. The resemblance needs to be clear. A few years ago, when **lapides** = 'stones' appeared in an Unseen, a number of candidates, with the French **lapin** in mind, translated the word as 'rabbits'.

Finally, you may be able to guess the meaning of a word correctly after you have got the rest of the Unseen translated and can see the context in which the word occurs. You will then have your last chance of filling in any gaps that you have had to leave. Obviously your chance of guessing correctly depends on what success you have had with the rest of the Unseen. A gap in rubbish will be filled in by rubbish. A gap in a translation which has been carefully worked out has an excellent chance of being filled in correctly by an intelligent guess. But before this stage is reached, you have got to translate at least the greater part of the Unseen. Given that you know, or can work out, the meanings of most of the words, you have got to tackle the syntax, i.e., work out how the words are strung together.

Obviously any Unseen consists of a number of sentences marked out by punctuation. Each sentence is a unit – and it is highly important for you to realise that examiners will mark it as a unit. This means that, *if you translate a sentence correctly, you will get the whole of the marks allocated to that sentence, no matter what rubbish you may have written elsewhere*. Sentences may be either Simple, i.e., without any subordinate clauses, or Compound, i.e., with at least one subordinate clause, and often with more than one. Compound sentences will set you your main problems; but the idea of this book is to introduce you gradually to the main types of subordinate clause. The simple sentence – and it is safe to say that all Unseens contain two or three of these – offers no problems apart from vocabulary, provided that a few simple rules for translation are observed. It is worth while to run through these rules, simply because, elementary though they are, they are much too often ignored by O-Level candidates.

All simple sentences contain a subject and a verb. (The only difference here between Latin and English is that, in English, the subject – except with imperatives – is always visible in the sentence; whereas, in Latin, a subject which is one of the personal pronouns, such as 'I', 'he', 'they', etc., is usually invisible, i.e., it is 'contained in the verb' and is shown only by the verb-ending.) They may or may not contain an object. Although in your English translation the subject will come before the verb, *don't look for it first in the Latin*. Look for the *verb*, since it will *always* give you information about the subject. If the verb is in any person other than the third, you need look no further for the subject – which must be, according to the person of the verb, one of the following: 'I', 'you' (singular), 'we', 'you' (plural). (These personal pronouns will only be shown in the Latin as **ego**, **tu**, etc., if there is special emphasis on them.) If the verb is in the third person singular or plural, you have got to look for the subject. If the verb is in the third person singular, it may still contain the subject within itself, i.e., 'he', 'she', or 'it', according to the sense. But the subject may also be some nominative singular noun which *is* expressed in the Latin and which you must look for. Similarly, if the verb is in the third person plural, the subject may be 'they' (unexpressed), but it may also be some nominative plural noun which *is* expressed in the Latin and which you must look for. In any sentence, therefore, the verb, by its verb-endings, will either provide you with a subject which is unexpressed in the Latin ('I', 'you', 'he', etc.), or will guide you to a subject which is expressed in the Latin in front of you. Remember that extra guidance is given you by verbs in the passive voice and by deponent verbs, provided that their tense happens to be one of the so-called compound tenses, i.e.

those which are formed by combining the perfect participle of the verb with tenses of **sum**. Since, in such tenses, the participle has to agree in gender as well as number with the subject, you are given an extra bit of information about the subject: its gender. E.g., **Secutae sunt complures dies tempestates** = '*Storms followed for several days*' (the only possible meaning, since **secutae** shows that a feminine plural subject is required – and **dies** in the plural is always masculine). The verb will also tell you whether there is likely to be an object in the sentence. If the verb is in the passive voice or if you are quite certain that it is intransitive, don't bother to look for an object. There isn't one – and if you do find one, you are making havoc of the sentence. If the verb is in the active voice and is transitive, it will probably have an object. In a simple sentence, this object will be a noun or pronoun in the accusative singular or plural. Don't forget that there are a number of Latin verbs which are followed by an object (of sorts) which is not in the accusative. The majority of such verbs are those that are followed by a dative. I say an object 'of sorts' because technically such verbs are intransitive and the object is not a true object; but for purposes of translation you have got to take it as the object.

By following these simple directions, you are now able to split the sentence up into subject, verb, and object (if any). All that remains to be done, before you write out a translation, is to group round these components anything that goes with them: e.g., with subject and object, any adjective(s) in agreement with either, any noun in apposition to either, any genitive dependent on either; and, with the verb, any adverb or adverbial phrase. Example: **Itaque custodes, viri ferocissimi, meae uxoris fratres ad urbis portam mox mittent**. Here, the verb **mittent**, being third person plural, tells you that the subject *must* be either 'they' or some nominative plural noun. Being a transitive verb, it also tells you that there is likely to be an object. Nouns which could be nominative plural are **custodes**, **fratres**, and **viri**. Try **custodes** first, since in any Latin sentence the subject usually (though not always) comes early. You get 'guards will send' (unless you bungle the tense of the verb). To complete the sense, an object is plainly needed. **Viri** won't serve, since, if it isn't nominative plural, it is genitive singular. **Custodes** and **fratres** could both be nominative or accusative plural. In itself, this means that 'guards will send brothers' and 'brothers will send guards' are both possible translations. You must therefore look around to see if there is anything else which will help you to decide between these two translations. You have got the help that you need, provided that you know enough about punctuation. **Viri ferocissimi**, clearly a noun + adjective phrase, could be a genitive singular attached to **custodes**: 'the guards of the very fierce man'. But it could also be a nominative plural, in apposition to **custodes**: 'the guards, very fierce men'. It is only the punctuation – the fact that the phrase is between commas – which tells you that it must be in apposition to **custodes**. (It is the custom to punctuate Latin in the same way as English, and, as in English, a phrase or noun in apposition usually follows the noun to which it is in apposition: e.g., 'Socrates, a very wise man', **Socrates, vir sapientissimus**.) You now know with certainty that **custodes** is the subject, because **viri ferocissimi** must be grouped with it as a nominative plural in apposition. You now know with certainty that **fratres** is the object. The grouping of the rest of the words is now easy. **Meae uxoris** can only be a genitive singular grouped with **fratres**. **Ad urbis portam** and **mox** – an adverbial phrase and an adverb – must be grouped with the verb. Notice the position of the genitive singular **urbis**. In the word-order of Latin, a genitive grouped with a noun governed by a preposition is commonly sandwiched between the preposition and the noun which it governs: 'to (of the city) gate' = 'to the gate of the city'. You are left with the connecting-word **itaque** which begins the sentence. It means 'therefore' or 'and so', and marks a rather stronger causal connection than **atque**. You will find both these words as well as **mox** = 'soon', in Appendix B. The whole sentence is now ready for translation: 'And so the guards, very fierce men, will soon send my wife's brothers to the gate of the city.'

This example of a simple sentence has been set down here as an isolated item, and its meaning has been worked out without help from whatever its context might have been. But the sentences (whether simple or compound) which you meet in an Unseen or a Comprehension Passage are *not* isolated items but parts of a coherent 'story'; and their context, if you use it intelligently, will help you to get their meaning. E.g., in the example we have just looked at, the context would have shown you whether the subject of **mittent** was **custodes** or **fratres**. None the less, if you don't see clearly how the words are strung together, you are not going to avoid 'syntactical' mistakes which, from their nature, are likely to involve more than one word.

We can now begin to think about compound sentences. These are sentences which contain a main clause and one or more subordinate clauses. Remember that, in these clauses, whether main or subordinate, you will find the pattern, already noted in the simple sentence, of subject-with-any-attachments, verb-with-any-attachments, object (if any)-with-any-attachments.

Subordinate clauses vary considerably in difficulty; and you will be tackling the more difficult specimens one at a time. Regarding the easier types of subordinate clause, Latin, like English, uses these so frequently that any Unseen, unless it has been made so childishly simple as to be valueless for O-Level candidates, is likely to include a few specimens. Commonest are Relative Clauses, Causal Clauses, Temporal Clauses; and these three types of subordinate clauses are best dealt with at once.

Of the three, the trickiest to translate from English to Latin is the Relative Clause; but it should cause you little difficulty when you are translating from Latin to English. Remember that all relative clauses are descriptive, i.e., they describe some person(s) or thing(s). The commonest way of describing persons or things is to use an adjective or adjectives: 'Julius is a cruel boy.' But adjectives can only give us a *general* description; and, if we want to describe a *particular* way in which Julius is cruel, the commonest way is to use a relative clause: 'Julius is the boy who killed the cat.' Another *particular* description of Julius might be: 'Julius is the boy whom the R.S.P.C.A. prosecuted.' From these examples two important things can be seen. a) A relative clause must be 'related' to someone or something, i.e., to some person or thing described by the clause. (This person or thing is called the antecedent – a cumbrous but handy word.) b) In English, the relative pronoun in a clause describing a person is 'who' when it is the subject of its clause, as in 'the boy who killed the cat', but 'whom' when it is the object, as in 'the boy whom the R.S.P.C.A. prosecuted'. It is b) which causes the trouble when you are translating from English to Latin; for you must then remember that, although the relative pronoun **qui, quae, quod** has to agree with its antecedent in gender and number, its case depends on the job which it is doing in its own clause, i.e., on whether it is subject, object, indirect object, governed by a preposition, etc. When you are

10

translating from Latin to English, you have a much easier task. All you need to remember is that, if the Latin relative pronoun is in the nominative case and *its antecedent is a person or persons*, you will translate it as 'who'; and that, if it is in any other case *except the genitive*, you will translate it as 'whom', e.g., 'whom we saw', 'to whom we gave the book', 'by whom we were seen'. The genitive is the exception simply because the English relative pronoun 'who', besides having an accusative 'whom', has a genitive 'whose': 'Julius is the boy whose book I borrowed.'

The question whether to use 'who' or 'whom' only arises when the antecedent is a person or persons. If the antecedent is a thing or things, the relative pronoun in English is 'which', no matter what case it is in: 'the river which flows through London is the Thames'; 'the river which you crossed was wide'; 'the words to which you refer were certainly rude.' Strictly speaking, 'which' has no genitive 'whose'. It is correct to say: 'the river on the banks of which London was built is the Thames.' It is less correct, though common usage and entirely acceptable, to say: 'the river on whose banks . . . .'.

Here are three examples of relative clauses, all taken from Caesar's *Gallic War*. a) **Summa imperii traditur Camulogeno, qui propter singularem scientiam rei militaris ad eum honorem evocatus est** (B.G. VII, 57) = '*The supreme command was handed over to Camulogenus, who was called to that distinction on account of his unique knowledge of warfare*.' (The antecedent is in the dative, the relative is in the nominative.) b) **Interim Teutomarus, cuius pater ab senatu nostro amicus erat appellatus, ad eum pervenit** (B.G. VII, 29) = '*Meanwhile Teutomarus, whose father had been called friend by our senate, came to him*.' (Antecedent in the nominative, relative in the genitive.) c) **Flumen est Arar, quod in Rhodanum influit** (B.G. I, 12) = '*The river is the Arar, which flows into the Rhone*.' (Antecedent and relative both in the nominative.)

Translators from Latin to English should have no trouble with straightforward relative clauses of the type just illustrated. On the other hand, there is a particular use of the relative which they have got to understand, but which translators from English to Latin can avoid. This is the Latin usage called the Connecting Relative. By using the relative pronoun, Latin authors often link a sentence closely to the sentence which precedes it. The kind of thing which they do can occasionally be found in English: 'I can see that you are a

complete fool. *Which* being so, I want nothing more to do with you.'
In this example, although 'which being so' is acceptable English,
much more usual English would be 'this being so'. But of course
'which' provides a closer link than 'this'; and it is just this type of
close linkage which the Latin writers are fond of using. English
writers seldom use it; and, although 'which being so' does happen to
be acceptable English, you will find that a translation of the Latin
connecting relative by the English relative will almost invariably
sound ridiculous. Instead, you will need to translate it by an English
demonstrative ('this', 'that', 'these', 'those'), as the following
examples show. a) **Caesar omnem senatum ad se convenire
principumque liberos obsides ad se adduci iussit. Quae omnia
ab his diligenter facta sunt** (B.G. II, 5) = (literally) *'Caesar ordered
all the senate to assemble to him and the children of the chiefs to be brought to
him as hostages. All which things were carefully done by them.'* 'All which
things' is certainly not acceptable as English; and 'all these/those
things' must be substituted. Caesar himself, if he had not wanted the
close linkage which **quae** provides, would have written **haec/ea/illa
omnia. b) Ipse Britanniam attigit atque ibi hostium copias
conspexit. Cuius loci haec erat natura** (B.G. IV, 23) = (literally)
*'He himself reached Britain and there caught sight of the forces of the enemy.
Of which area this was the nature.'* As in the previous example, English
requires a demonstrative instead of the relative: 'This was the nature
of that area.'

We have not quite done with the connecting relative. You will
find that it is used most frequently of all in causal and temporal
clauses. Since this particular use of it is one which, when it is set at O
Level, is bungled by some 30% of candidates, we shall have to look
at further examples within the framework of these clauses.

Causal Clauses are those which, in English, are introduced by
'because' or 'since'. In Latin, they are usually introduced by **quod** or
cum. Quod is nearly always followed by a verb in the indicative (an
instance, in one of the Unseens in this book, of its use with the
subjunctive is explained to you in a foot-note to the Unseen). The
only snag with **quod** is that a careless translator can confuse it with
the nominative or accusative neuter singular of the relative pronoun,
which of course is also **quod**. To eliminate the possibility of this
confusion, some text-books prefer to use **quia** = 'because'; but **quia**
is not much used by Latin authors (Caesar never uses it at all). **Quod**

is what you can expect to see, and, in any sentence in which it occurs, you must look at the Latin carefully in order to decide whether it is the conjunction = 'because', or the relative = 'which'. There is no real problem here. If it is the relative, there must be, in the sentence, some neuter singular noun or pronoun as its antecedent; and of course the sense, too, will be your guide. Take an example already looked at: **Flumen est Arar, quod in Rhodanum influit**. Here, a) there is a neuter singular noun **flumen** which is a possible antecedent for **quod**; b) the sense shows that this noun *must* be the antecedent of **quod** the relative, since **quod** the conjunction makes no sense at all – the river isn't the Arar *because* it flows into the Rhone. Take another example: **Dumnorix Helvetiis erat amicus, quod ex civitate Orgetorigis filiam in matrimonium duxerat** (B.G. I, 9) = '*Dumnorix was friendly to the Helvetii, because he had married the daughter of Orgetorix from that state*.' Here, a) there is no neuter singular noun or pronoun as a possible antecedent for **quod**; b) the substitution of 'which' for 'because' wrecks the sense.

Cum is one of the commonest Latin conjunctions. The chief snags about it are a) it is usually followed by a subjunctive; b) it can mean either 'since' or 'when'; c) it can be – and in the O-Level examination often is – confused with the preposition **cum** = 'with'. As regards a), the subjunctive is basic to Latin (as it is to Italian, though much less so to French), and you will not get far with any Latin writer unless you can identify the subjunctive tenses correctly. If you can't do this, there is no point in attempting any of the Unseens in this book, since the very first Unseen contains three examples of **cum** + subjunctive. Once the subjunctive has been identified – and, with **cum**, pluperfect subjunctives are by far the commonest – there is no further problem, since the subjunctive is translated exactly as though it were the corresponding tense of the indicative. As regards b), whether **cum** has to be translated by 'since' or 'when' depends on the context in which it occurs – and we will look at an example or two in a minute. As regards c), **cum** = 'with' is followed by an ablative. Usually, this is enough of a give-away; but occasionally you find **cum** + subjunctive and, in the same clause, you find an ablative which is nothing to do with **cum** but happens to be following it. E.g., **Quorum timor cum fremitu et concursu significaretur, milites nostri in castra irruperunt** (B.G. IV, 14) = '*Since their fear*' (literally: 'fear of which men' – connecting relative) *'was revealed by uproar and bustling, our troops broke into the camp.'* In this example, **cum** is in no way connected with the ablatives **fremitu** and **concursu** which *happen* to follow it. (They are instrumental ablatives = 'by', not 'with'.) The word with which **cum** is connected is the subjunctive **significaretur**.

Notice that, in this last example, **cum** could equally well be translated as 'when': it was 'when their fear was revealed' that 'our troops broke in'. In fact, examples in which 'when' would have to be marked wrong are not common. Far commoner are examples in which 'since' is plainly wrong and 'when' is plainly right. **Cum**, therefore, provides a handy bridge between causal and temporal clauses. But before we look at temporal clauses, **quoniam** = 'since' deserves a mention. Like **quia**, it is not a common word, but you may come across it. It presents no problem, as it always means 'since' and it is usually followed by an indicative.

Temporal Clauses, as their name implies, are time-clauses. They are introduced in Latin by such conjunctions as **ubi** = 'when', **postquam** = 'after', **antequam/priusquam** = 'before', **simul atque/simulac** = 'as soon as'. Since these conjunctions are normally followed by a verb in the indicative (at O Level various complications are excluded), you should have no trouble with these time-clauses. Here are examples of the use of **ubi**, **postquam**, and **simul atque**, the example of **ubi** being combined with a connecting relative. a) **Quod ubi Caesar animadvertit, naves longas paulum removeri iussit** (B.G. IV, 25) = *'When Caesar noticed this, he ordered the war-ships to be withdrawn a little.'* b) **Postquam id animadvertit, copias suas in proximum collem subducit** (B.G.I, 24) = *'After Caesar noticed this he withdrew his forces to the nearest hill.'* (Here, Caesar does not use the connecting relative which he used in a). He may have felt that **id**, though not providing as close a linkage, was more emphatic.) c) **Hostes, simul atque se ex fuga receperunt, statim ad Caesarem legatos de pace miserunt** (B.G. IV, 27) = *'The enemy, as soon as they recovered from their flight, at once sent ambassadors to Caesar regarding peace.'*

Cum = 'when' needs attention. Whenever an instance of it occurs in an O-Level Unseen, a lot of candidates lose a mark by writing 'since' – presumably because, having learned, correctly, that **cum** can mean either 'when' or 'since', they don't realise that there are plenty of instances in which it means 'when', *and only 'when'*. In

14

fact, the realisation that there *are* such instances ought to be enough to prevent any mistake. When these instances occur, they are always obvious enough to any candidate who takes the trouble to think about the meaning of the Latin, as the following two examples will show. a) **Cum iam extremi essent in prospectu, equites a Q. Atrio ad Caesarem venerunt** (B.G. V, 10) = '*When the hindmost (of the enemy) were already in sight, cavalry came to Caesar from Quintus Atrius.*' Here, as the context clearly shows, the **cum**-clause simply indicates the time of the cavalry's arrival. These cavalry are messengers who have come to tell Caesar that his beached ships have been badly damaged by a storm. They arrive at an inopportune moment – just when Caesar is catching up with the enemy. Substitution of 'since' for 'when' wrecks the sense by producing the absurd idea that the cavalry arrived *because* Caesar was catching up with the enemy. b) **Quae cum appropinquarent Britanniae, tempestas subito coorta est** (B.G. IV, 28) = '*When these were approaching Britain, a storm suddenly sprang up.*' 'These', in fact, are ships; and **quae**, a connecting relative, refers to **naves** in a previous sentence. Again, substitution of 'since' for 'when' wrecks the sense – the storm did not spring up *because* the ships were approaching Britain. It should now be clear to you that, in order to make sure that you translate **cum** correctly, you have got to look at the sense of the passage which you are translating. You can then decide on the translation which fits the sense; and you will have your first opportunity to do this when you tackle the **cum**-clauses in the first Unseen in this book.

Accusative and infinitive

The first two Unseens differ to a considerable extent, as printed here, from the form in which they appeared when set for O Level. While a great deal of the original wording has been retained, the differences are that they have been adapted to illustrate the Accusative and Infinitive construction, and that all other major constructions have been eliminated. Six examples of the accusative and infinitive construction – hereafter, for reasons of space, abbreviated to acc. and inf. – appear in the first Unseen and seven in the second, as against three and two in the original versions. There is no doubt about the importance of this construction. You will very seldom meet an O-Level Unseen which does not contain at least one example of it, and you may well find three or four or more in a single Unseen. Since the same cannot be said of any other construction, acc. and inf. merits, and will get here, the maximum of attention.

The acc. and inf. construction is used in Latin with 'verbs of saying and thinking', i.e., with any verb which indicates some form of speech (e.g., 'say', 'declare', 'inform', 'deny', 'announce', 'reply', 'persuade') or some form of mental process (e.g., 'think', 'know', 'believe', 'hear', 'understand', 'realise', 'see'). Some of these 'verbs of thinking' can be followed by an acc. and inf. in English. It is grammatically correct to say: 'I believe him to be a fool', 'we know them to be rogues', 'I understand her to be lying.' (I have used the personal pronouns 'him', 'them', 'her' in these examples because these pronouns, having both nominative and accusative forms, show clearly that in English, as in Latin, only the accusative can be used in this construction. 'I know she to be a liar' is good dialect in some areas but it is bad English anywhere.) But although a few 'verbs of thinking' can be used with an acc. and inf. in English, it is plain fact a) that the construction isn't often used, and b) that with most verbs of *saying* it is never used at all. 'I believe the boy to be a fool' is correct English; 'I say the boy to be a fool' is not. In English the second of these two sentences has got to be: 'I say that the boy is a fool'; the first sentence, though grammatical as it stands, will much more usually be: 'I believe that the boy is a fool.' In Latin, the acc. and inf. is always used in clauses of this type; and our two examples will read thus: **Credo/dico puerum stultum esse**. The difference, therefore, between English and Latin is as follows. In English, 'verbs of saying and thinking' are mostly followed by a clause introduced by the conjunction 'that', which is itself followed by a noun or pronoun in the nominative + a verb in the indicative + an object (if required). E.g., 'The messenger says that the Romans are sending help.' In Latin there will be no conjunction; the noun or pronoun, which in English is in the nominative as the subject of the 'that-clause', will be in the accusative; and the verb, which in the English 'that-clause' is indicative, will be in the infinitive. E.g., **Nuntius dicit Romanos mittere auxilium**. There is no mystery here. The translator from Latin to English has to do three simple things: a) supply the word 'that' (for which, of course, there is no equivalent in the Latin); b) translate the Latin accusative as though it were a nominative (not much of a problem, since in English, pronouns apart, there are no separate forms for nominative and accusative); c) translate the Latin infinitive as though it were an indicative.

The examples used so far have been very simple ones, with all verbs in the present tense. Keeping the *main* verb in the present tense, let us see what variants are possible in the 'that-clause', using the last example 'The messenger says . . .'. Plainly, just two: instead of being in the present tense, the verb could be in the past or the future, i.e., 'The messenger says that the Romans sent/have sent/did send help' (past); 'will send/are going to send help' (future). As one would expect, Latin, which uses infinitives where English is using indicatives, naturally uses a perfect infinitive for past time and a future infinitive for future time; i.e., **Nuntius dicit Romanos auxilium misisse** = '*The messenger says that the Romans sent/have sent/did send help*'; **Nuntius dicit Romanos auxilium missuros esse** = '*The messenger says that the Romans will send/are going to send help*.'

The three infinitives of **mitto** which we have now seen are all active; but all transitive verbs (such as **mitto**) also have three corresponding infinitives – present, perfect and future – which are passive. And at this point it has to be said that, when you are translating an acc. and inf., having identified the construction and therefore having made a good start, you must be very careful to get the tense of the infinitive right – bearing in mind that, if the Latin verb is transitive, you have a possible six infinitives to play with, three active and three passive. Latin grammar, as such, is not within the scope of this book; but the acc. and inf. construction is of such vital importance that, in this instance, we can take a closer-than-usual look at the grammar which is involved. Before tackling even the first Unseen in this book, make sure, by revision in a grammar book or something similar, that you are certain of recognising the present, perfect, and future infinitive, active and passive, of the four regular conjugations. Remember that these set a pattern for the formation of infinitives which is followed by *all* Latin verbs except for the very small handful of true irregulars, i.e., **sum** and its compounds, **volo**, **nolo**, **malo**, **eo** and its compounds, **fero** and its compounds, **fio**. Even these irregulars follow the regular pattern for the formation of all their infinitives except the present. As these irregular present infinitives are in very common use and are an essential part of your vocabulary, check them over. In general, Latin infinitives are not difficult to identify. Don't overlook the usual aids, i.e., that *all* perfect infinitives active end in **-isse**; that *all* future infinitives active are revealed by **-urus esse** (**-urus** is of course declinable, and, in the acc. and inf. construction, can naturally appear only with an accusative ending); that *all* future infinitives passive are revealed by their formation: the supine of the verb (which is a word ending in an unalterable **-um**) + **iri**. One specific warning: while the other three conjugations form their present infinitives passive by altering the final **-e** of the active form to **-i** (e.g., **amare** becomes **amari**), **regere** (third conjugation) does not become **regeri** but **regi**. This present infinitive passive, common of course to all third conjugation verbs as well as to hybrids of the **capio** type, is the one which O-Level candidates most often fail to recognise – with unfortunate results, though perhaps with some excuse, since such words as **regi**, **capi**, **duci**, **instrui**, look more like nouns than verbs, and indeed **regi** and **duci** are also the dative singulars of **rex** and **dux**. The first Unseen in this book contains the following six infinitives in the acc. and inf. construction: **posse, vicisse, superesse**, **discessisse**, **rediturum esse**, **futurum esse**. You should have no difficulty in picking out, from these six, two present, two perfect, and two future infinitives, all active. In the second Unseen, you will find, in the acc. and inf. construction, three present infinitives (one of which is passive), three perfect infinitives (two of which are passive), one future infinitive passive.

Having identified an infinitive, you have still got to translate it correctly as regards its tense. (I am assuming that you know the basic meaning of the word which is in the infinitive.) If the main verb is in the present tense, there is, as we have already seen, no problem at all: a Latin present infinitive is translated by an English present indicative, a Latin perfect infinitive by an English past tense, a Latin future infinitive by an English future tense. E.g., **Putamus Caesarem in urbe esse/fuisse/futurum esse** = '*We think that Caesar is/was/will be in the city*.' If the main verb is in a past tense – as are the majority of main verbs which you meet in O-Level Unseens – a bit of care is needed. In English 'We think that Caesar is in the city' becomes, when we put the main verb into a past tense, 'We thought that Caesar *was* in the city.' In Latin, however, the present infinitive is retained: **Putavimus Caesarem in urbe esse**. The reason for this becomes obvious if, instead of translating by a 'that-clause', we use the acc. and inf. in English. Correct English then is: 'We thought Caesar to be in the city' – an exact parallel to the Latin. Remember therefore that, after a past main verb, a Latin present infinitive has to be translated by a past tense in the English 'that-clause'. Notice, too, that after a past main verb a Latin perfect infinitive is translated by an English pluperfect, and a Latin future infinitive is translated by 'would' instead of 'will':

Scivimus Caesarem flumen transiisse = '*We knew that Caesar had crossed the river*.' (Literally: 'We knew Caesar to have crossed'.)
Putavi puerum rediturum esse = '*I thought that the boy would return*.' (Literally: 'I thought the boy to be going-to-return'.)

Of three particular snags regarding acc. and inf. which bother translators from English to Latin, only one gives any trouble to translators from Latin to English, but perhaps all three are worth mentioning – if only for the benefit of those who choose to write Latin. a) There are four English verbs, 'hope', 'promise', 'threaten', 'swear', which in English can be, and usually are, followed by a present infinitive. (You will find the Latin equivalent of one of these verbs in the first Unseen.) In Latin, this English present infinitive is always rendered by an accusative and *future* infinitive. E.g., 'I promise to go' becomes, in Latin, **Promitto me iturum esse** = '*I promise that I will go*.' Since this last translation is just as good English as 'I promise to go', the translator from Latin to English has no problem here. b) In Latin, it is not permissible to use **dico** followed by a **non** in the acc. and inf. clause. Instead of **dico . . . non**, **nego** (= 'deny') is used. Again, there is no problem for the translator from Latin to English, because there is nothing wrong with a literal translation: **Negavimus urbem captum iri** = '*We said that the city would not be taken*' or '*We denied that the city would be taken.*' Either translation is acceptable. c) The translator from English to Latin has to be careful with a translation of 'he', 'she', 'they', when one of these words is the subject of an acc. and inf. clause. The rule is that **se** is used in Latin for all three words, provided that they refer back to the subject of the main verb. E.g., '*This boy says that he can run*' = **Hic puer dicit se posse currere**; '*The foolish girl thought that she was wise*' = **Stulta puella se sapientem esse putavit**; '*Those girls/boys know that they will be sent home*' = **Illae puellae/illi pueri se domum missum iri sciunt**. As a translator from Latin to English, you can't escape involvement here. You have got to understand that **se** in an acc. and inf. can mean 'he' or 'she' or 'they', and that the subject of the main verb shows you which one to choose. When the reference is *not* to the subject of the main verb, Latin uses **eum** for 'he', **eam** for 'she', **eos** for 'they' if 'they' are male, **eas** for females. There is obviously no problem for the translator when one or other of these words is used; and one simple example will suffice: **Putamus eum/eam esse sapientem** = '*We think that he/she is wise.*' The first two Unseens will give you practice in the translation of **se**. In the second Unseen, you will find **eos** in the acc. and inf. construction. Don't think that this business of **se**, **eum**, etc. is just some Latin nonsense. When acc. and inf. is used in English, the parallel with Latin is exact: 'This boy thinks that he is clever' = 'This boy thinks himself to be clever'; 'We think that he is clever' = 'We think him to be clever.' If acc. and inf. were used universally in English, as it is in Latin, your job as a translator would certainly be an easier one. All the same, having now looked at any difficulties which this most important construction can cause, you ought to be able to tackle it confidently. You will certainly get plenty of practice, not merely thoughout the Unseens in this book, but in the Comprehension Passages as well.

Before you tackle the first Unseen, remember the importance a) of the Appendices, b) of advice already given you in *How to Tackle an Unseen*. In Appendix A, you will find the following words which occur in this Unseen: **acies**, **instruo**, **legatus**, **exercitus**, **supero**,

vinco, **proelium**, **interficio**, **discedo**, **copiae**, **resisto**, **castra**.
In Appendix B, you will find **supersum**, **audeo**, **redeo**, **atque**. In
How to Tackle an Unseen, you were shown how you can be helped by
English derivatives. In this first Unseen, English derivatives will
give you the meanings of: **annus**, **declaro**, **pestilentia**, **autumnus**,
consumo, **victor**. You were also shown how to get as much help as
possible from the English title of an Unseen. The title of this first
Unseen is, like all the English titles printed in this book, exactly as it
was when the Unseen was set at O Level. It shows you which to
choose out of the two possible meanings of **legatus**, and it (almost)
translates for you the first acc. and inf. of the six which occur in the
Unseen.

1 **Labienus, who had once served under Caesar but is now a
supporter of Pompeius, persuades Pompeius that Caesar can
easily be conquered**

    Cum Pompeius contra Caesarem aciem instruxisset,
Labienus, qui per decem annos in Gallia legatus Caesaris
fuerat, persuasit Pompeio exercitum Caesaris facile superari
posse. 'non debes putare' inquit 'hunc exercitum Gallos
vicisse. in Gallia adfui omnibus proeliis neque rem
incognitam[1] pronuntio. tibi declaro minimam partem illius
exercitus superesse. multi interfecti sunt; multos autumni
pestilentia in Italia consumpsit. cognovi multos domum
discessisse. hae copiae quas vides tibi resistere non audebunt.'
cum haec dixisset, iuravit[2] se nisi[3] victorem in castra non
rediturum esse. atque Pompeius ipse, cum verba Labieni
audivisset, pro certo habuit[4] se victorem futurum esse.

[1] **incognitus**, *unknown*   [2] **iurare**, *swear*   [3] **nisi**, *unless*
[4] **pro certo habere**, *be sure*

2 The appointment of a dictator at Rome causes the Praenestines to retreat to the river Allia

Nuntii Praenestinis dixerunt nullum exercitum Romae instrui neque ullum imperatorem creatum esse, cum discordia esset inter plebem ac senatores. tum Praenestinorum duces, qui occasionem sibi datam esse senserunt, magnis cum copiis ad portam Collinam progressi sunt. in urbe magna trepidatio fuit. multi cives 'ad arma' clamaverunt, cum urbem mox captum iri putarent; multi in moenia atque ad portas cucurrerunt. in tanto periculo omnes cives intellexerunt se debere verti ab seditione ad bellum. Cincinnatum igitur dictatorem creaverunt. Praenestini, cum existimarent se tali imperatori non posse resistere, a moenibus discesserunt. brevi tempore explorator Romanus nuntiavit eos haud procul Allia flumine castra posuisse.

Purpose clauses

The commonest way of expressing purpose in English is by the present infinitive. E.g., 'I come to bury Caesar'; 'some eat to live, others live to eat.' By contrast, Latin never uses the present infinitive in this way. Its commonest way of expressing purpose is by using **ut** = 'so that/in order that' followed by a verb in the subjunctive: **Venio ut Caesarem sepeliam** = (literally) *'I come in order that I may bury Caesar.'* Whilst 'in order that I may bury' lacks the punch of the original 'to bury', it is just as good grammatically – a fact which works handily for translators from Latin to English. For them, **ut** is there as a give-away; a subjunctive is there to clinch the matter – and they are always at liberty to translate the phrase literally. In present time, Latin uses the present subjunctive as in the example already quoted. In past time, Latin uses the imperfect subjunctive, and, in an English literal translation, 'may' must be replaced by 'might'. **Veni ut Caesarem sepelirem** = *'I came to bury Caesar'*, or (literally) *'I came in order that I might bury Caesar.'* In Latin, a purpose-**ut** is never followed by **non**. Instead of **ut . . . non**, **ne** is used. E.g., **Frumentum emo ne cives fame pereant** = *'I am buying corn in order that the citizens may not perish from hunger.'* The exact equivalent of **ne** is 'lest' – a word not much used these days, but if you wish to write 'lest the citizens perish' you certainly won't lose a mark. A troublesome feature of Latin purpose-clauses is that **ut** is sometimes replaced by the relative pronoun **qui, quae, quod**. This occurs in the following type of sentence: **Mittimus legatos qui pacem petant** = *'We are sending ambassadors to seek peace (who may seek peace)'*; **Faber advenit qui cloacam reficeret** = *'An engineer arrived to repair the sewer (who might repair the sewer).'* 'May' and 'might' will not, in fact, serve as translations this time because, when coupled thus with 'who', they merely indicate possibilities: the engineer might repair the sewer – or he might not. Therefore, when – as you certainly will – you meet **qui, quae, quod** + a verb in the subjunctive, you must recognise the purpose clause for what it is, and either translate it (if the sense fits, as it usually will) by an English present infinitive, 'to seek peace', 'to repair the sewer', or you must translate the plural **qui** by 'in order that they (may seek peace)' and

the singular **qui** by 'in order that he (might repair the sewer)'.
Unseen no. 3 contains five purpose clauses (and two acc. and inf.
clauses). In this Unseen, you meet the cumbersome Latin phrase
which means 'inform'. As the active and passive uses of this phrase
are essential to your O-Level Latin vocabulary, a word or two of
explanation isn't out of place. The usual Latin for 'I inform you' is **te
certiorem facio**, which literally means 'I make you more certain.'
Certiorem is an accusative singular, agreeing with **te**. An
accusative plural is of course equally possible, agreeing with a plural
object: **Dux milites certiores fecit** = (literally) *'The leader made the
soldiers more certain'* = *'The leader informed the soldiers.'* (*Don't*, on this
occasion, serve up the literal translation. In the O-Level
examination, you will be expected to know that the English
equivalent of this Latin phrase is 'inform'.) In the passive use of the
phrase, only the nominative forms **certior** (singular) and **certiores**
(plural) can be used, since **fio (fieri, factus sum)** is a true passive and
can take a complement but not an object: **Factus est certior** = *'He
has been/was informed.'*

As regards the vocabulary of Unseen no. 3, Appendix A gives
you the meanings of: **iter** and the phrase **magnum iter facere**,
appropinquare, **equitatus**, **eques**, **pauci**, **effugere**, **emittere**,
educere, **signum**, **proficisci**, **progredi**. Appendix B gives you
quoque. Apart from giving you **silentio**, English derivatives are
not much help and could lead you astray. **Clamor** refers to a
particular sort of noise, to which, in English, 'exclaim', not
'clamour', provides the clue. **Continuit** is not part of the verb
continuo, and does not mean 'continued'. To get the meaning, you
must remember that **contineo** (of which **continuit** is a part) is a
compound of **teneo** (the compounds of which all become **-tineo**).
In the phrase **iter suppressit**, 'suppressed', though literally correct,
is not a suitable translation. Think of a word of similar meaning
which will fit with your translation of **iter**.

Unseen no. 4 contains five purpose clauses, one of which is
introduced by **qui**. It also contains two acc. and inf. clauses. In
working this Unseen, you will find Appendix A of particular value.

3 Afranius' attempt to elude Caesar is unsuccessful

Cum magnum iter fecissent, milites Afrani montibus appropinquabant. hos montes intrare cupiebant, ut equitatum Caesaris effugerent; sed itineris labore fessi rem in posterum diem distulerunt[1], ut quiete[2] se reficerent. Caesar in proximo colle castra posuit. media circiter nocte, pauci milites, quos Afranius emiserat ut aquam invenirent, ab Caesaris equitibus capti sunt. ab his Caesar factus est certior Afranium silentio copias e castris educturum esse. quod cum cognovisset, signum dedit, ut statim suae quoque copiae proficiscerentur. sed cum propter strepitum[3] et clamorem sensisset Caesaris milites ex eo loco progredi, Afranius, ne nocte pugnare cogeretur[4], iter suppressit copiasque in castris continuit.

[1] **differre**, *postpone*   [2] **quies, -etis**, *rest*   [3] **strepitus**, *noise*
[4] **cogere**, *compel*

4 A force sent by King Juba to Utica is defeated by Curio's cavalry

Milites Curionis laborabant ut munitiones castrorum celeriter perficerent. sed equites ex statione nuntiaverunt magna auxilia equitum peditumque Uticam venire; eodemque tempore nubes[1] magna pulveris videbatur, et subito primum agmen erat in conspectu. Curio, qui pro certo habuit has copias a rege Iuba missas esse ut Romanos expelleret, praemisit equites qui primum impetum sustinerent. ipse, cum legiones a munitionibus deduxisset, aciem instruit, ne castra circumdarentur. equites proelium commiserunt atque in fugam coniecerunt omnia auxilia regis, quae perturbata erant, quod nullo ordine et sine timore iter fecerant. postero die Curio progressus est ut prope Uticam castra poneret.

[1] **nubes**, *cloud*

Indirect commands

Probably you are already acquainted with Direct Commands and Exhortations. These are found occasionally in O-Level Unseens, but they don't demand much space here, and the Latin usage – which requires of you nothing more than routine learning – can be summarised in a few lines: Latin imperative for all positive 2nd person commands, e.g., **mitte auxilium** = *'send help'*; if these are negatived, **noli**, or, if plural, **nolite**, + present infinitive, e.g., **noli pugnare** = *'don't fight'*; Latin present subjunctive for what grammarians call exhortations, i.e., the English use of 'let' in such expressions as 'let's go' = 'let us go' = (in Latin) **eamus**; exhortations are negatived by **ne**: *'let's not go'* = **ne eamus**.

Indirect Commands do demand a bit of space because a) they give trouble, b) they occur quite frequently in O-Level Unseens. They give trouble mainly because, in Latin, only two verbs, out of a dozen or so which can be followed by an indirect command, take a construction similar to that of English. English uses the accusative and present infinitive: 'We told *him to go home*.' (Notice, once again, that the use of the personal pronoun reveals the accusative. The nominative 'he' won't do.) English verbs which can be followed by this sort of accusative and present infinitive are: 'order', 'command', 'advise', 'persuade', 'ask', 'tell', 'entreat', 'encourage', 'exhort'. E.g., 'We encouraged the prisoner to eat'; 'I am asking you not to do this.' Notice that, in English, if a negative is required, it is simply put in front of the infinitive. In Latin, the only two verbs which are followed by an indirect command expressed, as in English, by the accusative and present infinitive are **iubeo** = 'order/command' and **veto** = 'forbid/order . . . not'. E.g., **Iussi eum domum ire** = *'I ordered him to go home.'* But Latin, in complete contrast with English usage, never puts a negative in front of a present infinitive in an indirect command, i.e., **iubeo** + **non** is never used. Instead, **veto** replaces **iubeo** and the negative. Thus **Vetui eum domum ire** = either *'I ordered him not to go home'* or *'I forbade him to go home.'* Either translation is correct.

These two verbs apart, all other Latin verbs which can introduce indirect commands (including **impero**, though it has the same meaning as **iubeo**) do so by the use of **ut**, or, if the indirect command is negatived, **ne**, + the present subjunctive in present time or the imperfect subjunctive in past time. E.g., **Eum monent ut ab urbe discedat** = '*They are warning him to leave the city*'; **Te rogo ne hoc facias** = '*I am asking you not to do this*'; **Persuasimus captivo ut ederet** = '*We persuaded the prisoner to eat*'; **Dux suos exhortatus est ne a barbaris terrerentur** = '*The leader exhorted his men not to be frightened by barbarians*.'

The similarity of indirect commands to purpose clauses is obvious – both use **ut** or **ne** with the present or imperfect subjunctive. It is a similarity which troubles O-Level candidates, who often translate indirect commands as though they were purpose clauses. Take one of the examples already given: **Te rogo ne facias** = '*I am asking you not to do this*.' This sentence, if set in an O-Level Unseen, would produce a very fair crop of the following mistranslations: 'I am asking you in order that you may not do this'; 'I am asking you lest you do this.' On an allocation of 2 marks for the phrase **ne hoc facias**, such mistranslations will lose 1. They are not so completely wrong as, say, 'by not doing this', but they are clear proof of failure to identify the indirect command. Unseen no. 5 will give you practice in such identification. It contains four indirect commands (one of which is introduced by **iubeo**); two purpose clauses (one of which is introduced by **qui**); and one acc. and inf.

27

Use of participles

In Unseens nos. 1–4, Participles have been eliminated, but they are in fact very common and their use in Latin must be thoroughly understood. Any transitive Latin verb has the following three participles: present and future (both active), perfect (passive). Take **rego** as an example. Present: **regens, –entis** = '(while) ruling'; future: **recturus-a-um** = '(being) about to rule'; perfect: **rectus-a-um** = '(having been) ruled'. All transitive verbs follow this general pattern; intransitive verbs, having no passive, have no perfect participle; deponent verbs follow the pattern, except that their perfect participles are active in meaning, e.g., **conatus-a-um** (from **conor** = 'try') means 'having tried'.

All participles are adjectives – which means that they have got to agree with some noun or pronoun. But they are *verbal* adjectives – which means that they imply action, and are not merely descriptive. Compare two sentences: a) **Illi antiqui libri sunt mei** = '*Those old books are mine*'; b) **Illi libri inventi a te sunt mei** = '*Those books found by you are mine.*' In a), the adjective **antiqui** (= 'old') is merely descriptive; in b), the verbal adjective **inventi** (= 'found'), while being descriptive, as any adjective must be, implies action. Compare another two sentences: a) **Puer stultus in flumen cecidit** = '*The stupid boy fell into the river*'; b) **Ambulans in ripa, puer in flumen cecidit** = '*Walking on the bank, the boy fell into the river.*' In a) the adjective 'stupid' is merely descriptive; in b) the verbal adjective 'walking' describes what the boy was doing when he fell. The future participle is the least common of the three Latin participles. Here is an example of its use: **Rediturus domum brevi tempore, puer sapiens ad matrem epistolam misit** = '*Being about to return home shortly, the wise boy sent a letter to his mother.*' Here, the boy is described in two ways: a) by a verbal adjective **rediturus** = 'being about to return' (English, having no future participle, has no one-word equivalent of a Latin future participle); b) by a merely descriptive adjective **sapiens** = 'wise'. (There may have been a further connection between the two sorts of adjective: the boy was wise in writing a letter because, being about to return, he wanted mother to have the house ready for him.) One more example of a participle is needed: the perfect participle, active in meaning, of a deponent verb:

**Profecti prima luce, milites, cum ad castra vesperi
advenissent, defessi erant** = '*Having set out at first light, the soldiers,
when they had reached camp in the evening, were tired out*.' The adjective
defessi = 'tired out' is merely descriptive; the verbal adjective
profecti (prima luce) = 'having set out (at first light)' describes the
soldiers by telling us of their action: they were early starters. In
Latin, as in English, a participle may be side by side with the word
with which it agrees, just as it was in our first example: **libri inventi**
= 'books found'. On the other hand, and rather more frequently,
several words will intervene, as in **rediturus domum brevi
tempore, puer** etc. This means that you must be careful to identify
correctly, not merely the participle itself, but also the word with
which it agrees. Unseen no. 5 will give you practice in both these
things. It contains eight participles (one future, two present, five
perfect – two of which are deponent). Only two of these participles
are side by side with the word with which they agree. This Unseen
illustrates the straightforward use of participles as verbal adjectives;
and the particular snag involving participles, the construction called
the Ablative Absolute, has been deliberately omitted for the
moment.

For Unseen no. 5 you need to brush up on your Latin numerals
and on the Latin use of an accusative for extent of time and extent of
space. Appendix A will be helpful with the vocabulary. Appendix B
will give you **eo, moror, cohortor** and **cohors**. **Deficio** is not a
common word but you should be able to get its meaning from an
English derivative. **Interrumpo** does not, here, mean 'interrupt'
and **eruptio** does not mean 'eruption', but both words are in
Appendix A.

Unseen no. 6 contains a mixture of the constructions so far
covered. This Unseen is a greater test of general vocabulary than any
of the preceding ones.

5 Domitius requests help from Pompeius when Caesar besieges him in Corfinium

Caesar unum diem moratus Corfinium contendit. eo cum venisset, cohortes quinque a Domitio ex oppido missae interrumpebant pontem tria milia passuum ab oppido distantem. cum proelium commissum esset, milites Domiti celeriter a ponte repulsi in oppidum se receperunt. Caesar, exspectans eruptionem, prope moenia castra posuit. tum Domitius, perterritus, ad Pompeium nuntios misit qui eum rogarent ut auxilium mitteret. Pompeium certiorem fecit non solum triginta cohortes sed etiam ducentos senatores in summum periculum venisse. suos cohortatus ne animo deficerent, Domitius iussit milites disponi in moenibus ut oppidum defendi posset. interim Caesar, Corfinium oppugnaturus, suis imperavit ut castra munirent.

6 On the advice of Aristides, the Athenians reject unheard Themistocles' plan to destroy the fleet of the Lacedaemonians

Athenienses Lacedaemoniique socii fuerant in bello contra Persas gesto. post sociorum victoriam Themistocles dixit in contione[1] se habere consilium reipublicae utile, sed nolle id apud omnes cives declarare. rogavit igitur populum ut aliquem sibi daret cum quo id consilium communicaret. datus est Aristides. huic ille dixit classem Lacedaemoniorum, non procul in litore subductam, clam incendi posse. quod cum Aristides audivisset, in contionem venit dixitque consilium Themistoclis utilissimum esse sed minime honestum[2]. itaque Athenienses, quod non honestum esset, id ne utile quidem[3] esse putaverunt, totamque eam rem, quam non audierant, repudiaverunt.

[1] **contio**, *an assembly*   [2] **honestus**, *honourable*
[3] **ne . . . quidem**, *not even*

Result clauses

If we use the old, but still prevalent, label for these clauses, we shall have to say that Consecutive Clauses express a consequence. It is simpler, and just as exact, to say that Result Clauses express a result. We can add to this statement of the obvious by saying first, that the result in these clauses is predetermined by what happens in the main clause; second, that the main clause will usually contain a 'sign-post' word which gives you an indication that a result clause may be on its way. Here are simple examples in English: a) 'He is so weak that he can't walk.' Inability to walk is the result of being so weak. The 'sign-post' word is 'so'. b) 'He used to work to such an extent that he was always tired.' A permanent state of tiredness resulted from such extensive work. The 'sign-post' word is 'such' in English, but in Latin the whole phrase 'to such an extent' will be represented by a single word, **adeo**. Just as, in English, a result clause is normally introduced by the conjunction 'that', so, in Latin, result clauses of the type which you will meet in O-Level Unseens are introduced by **ut** = 'that'. You *must* know all the 'sign-post' words. These are: **tam** and (much less commonly) **ita** = 'so', used with adjectives and adverbs, e.g., **tam fortis** = 'so brave', **tam celeriter** = 'so quickly'; **tantus -a -um** = 'so great/large/big'; **tot** (indeclinable) = 'so many'; **talis** = 'such/of such a kind'; **toties/totiens** = 'so often/so many times'; **ita/sic** = 'in such a way'; **adeo** = 'to such an extent'. Of course the presence of one of these 'sign-post' words in a Latin sentence does not, in itself, mean that a result clause is to follow. E.g., **Cur tot milites conscripsisti**? = '*Why did you enrol so many soldiers?*' – a question expecting, not a result clause, but an answer. (Keep this example in mind. When you work Unseen no. 7, you will find a rather similar phrase which *is* followed by a result clause.) But, when in a Latin sentence there is a 'sign-post' word in the main clause and when a subordinate clause follows which is introduced by **ut** and which has its verb in the subjunctive, it is very long odds that this subordinate clause is a result clause. As examples of result clauses will show, the subjunctive in these clauses has to be translated *as though it were an indicative*. Any introduction of 'may' or 'might' will wreck the sense. There is thus no parallel with purpose clauses, in which in any case only a present or an imperfect subjunctive can be used, and in which **ut** becomes **ne** if the clause is negatived. In result clauses, **ut** is unalterable and can be followed by **non** or any other negative such as **nemo**, **nullus**, **nunquam**, etc. As regards tenses, any tense of the subjunctive (including the so-called future subjunctive which you are soon to meet in the section on Indirect Questions) can be used if the sense requires it; but it is safe to say that the only subjunctives which you will meet in result clauses occurring in O-Level Unseens are the present, the imperfect, and the perfect. The following examples will show you that a result clause, once it has been spotted and any confusion with a purpose clause eliminated, is easy to translate.

Tam strenue laboravit ut iam fessus sit = '*He worked so hard that now he is tired*.' (*Present* tiredness the result of *past* effort.)

Vis tempestatis tanta fuerat ut nemo a castris discederet = '*The force of the storm had been so great that no one left the camp*.' (Imperfect subjunctive because a period of time was involved.)

Patrem adeo timuit ut domo discesserit = '*He feared his father to such an extent that he left home*.' (Perfect subjunctive to convey the once-and-for-all action of quitting home.)

Finally, here is an example which has not been manufactured but is taken from Caesar's *Gallic War*. On his first expedition to Britain, the ships carrying his cavalry run into trouble. Caesar writes: **Tanta tempestas subito coorta est ut nulla earum cursum tenere posset** (B.G. IV, 28) = '*So great a storm suddenly arose that none of these (ships) was able to hold course*.'

Unseen no. 7 contains four result clauses and no. 8 contains three. (All these result clauses are preceded by 'sign-post' words.) No. 7 will also give you plenty of further practice with participles: it contains eight instances. The title of this Unseen will give you the meaning of **obruerunt**. You will find **vix**, **via**, **cado**, **levis** in Appendix B. English derivatives will give you **truncus** and **fragmentum**. Since the glossary gives you **motus** = 'movement', you ought to be able to work out the meaning of **immotae**. Unseen no. 7 is very unusual in one respect: it contains no example of the acc. and inf. construction. You need not be disappointed for long: there are three examples of acc. and inf. in no. 8.

7 Romans are overwhelmed by falling trees which Gauls have partially severed

Consul Romanus, nomine Postumius, cum Gallos oppugnaret, pervenit ad silvam vastam per quam exercitum ducturus erat. haec silva tam densa erat ut via vix conspici posset. Galli arbores eius silvae circa viam ita inciderunt[1] ut immotae starent, sed motu[2] levi impulsae caderent. Postumius habebat duas legiones Romanas atque tot socios conscripserat ut viginti quinque milia armatorum in agros hostium duceret. ubi agmen silvam intravit, tum Galli impulerunt arbores incisas, quae cadentes viros equosque obruerunt, adeo ut vix decem homines ad salutem effugerent. nam cum multi truncis arborum fragmentisque ramorum[3] necati essent, Galli ceteros interfecerunt.

[1] **incido -ere, incidi, incisum**, *cut into*　　[2] **motus**, *movement*
[3] **ramus**, *branch*

8 Antony respects his old friendship with Atticus

Cum Caesar occisus esset, Brutus Cassiusque se receperunt ad Macedoniam. sed habuerunt exercitum tam parvum ut mox ab Antonio victi sint. cum Antonius victor Romam venisset, omnes putaverunt Atticum in tanto periculo esse ut ab Italia statim discedere deberet. Atticus enim erat amicus Ciceronis, oratoris clarissimi qui acriter Antonio restiterat. ac vero Antonius Ciceronem tam vehementer oderat ut non solum ei sed etiam omnibus eius amicis esset inimicus eosque vellet interficere. Meminerat tamen se ipsum paucis ante annis ab Attico adiutum esse. itaque Antonius, ut Attico persuaderet ut ad se sine timore veniret, misit ad eum epistolam sua manu scriptam. atque, ne in itinere Atticus oppugnaretur, Antonius misit praesidium quoque militum. Atticus igitur tutus Romam pervenit.

Indirect questions

You have now covered the three Latin subjunctive-constructions which occur frequently in O-Level Unseens. Indirect Questions occur a good deal less frequently than these three, but you can't afford to neglect them. It is assumed here that (apart, perhaps, from Double Direct Questions) you covered Direct Questions at an early stage of your study of Latin. Any direct question can be made indirect by making it dependent on some such verb as 'ask', 'know', 'discover', 'announce', 'inform', 'tell', 'remember', 'forget'. Examples: 'Who are you?' – direct question. 'I'm asking/I've discovered/I forget who you are' – the clause 'who you are' is an indirect question. In Latin, the verb of an indirect question is in the subjunctive. This is not much of a snag for the translator from Latin to English. As with the result clauses, all one needs is to spot the tense and then to translate it *as though it were an indicative*.

As with result clauses, the insertion of 'may' or 'might' will wreck the sense. Since, obviously, any indirect question must be introduced by a question-word, you need to brush up on these: words such as **quis**, **quid** ('who', 'what'), **quot** ('how many'), **quantus -a -um** ('how big/great'), **cur**, **quare** ('why'), **quomodo** ('how'), **quando** ('when'), and so on. All these, of course, can equally be used in direct questions. On the other hand – and this is a point which must be noted carefully – **num** (which you will have met introducing direct questions which expect the answer 'no') means 'whether' when it introduces an indirect question. As regards the tenses, not merely is indirect question the only construction in which all four tenses of the subjunctive are in regular use, but it is also the only construction in which, at O Level, you will meet the so-called future subjunctive. This future subjunctive is formed by using the future participle of the verb with **sim** (the present subjunctive of **sum**) or with **essem** (the imperfect subjunctive of **sum**), e.g., **facturus sim/essem**. For the translator, the difference is 'will' in the English when **sim** is used, and 'would' if it is **essem**, as the following examples will show: **Te rogo num tuus frater cras rediturus sit** = '*I'm asking you whether your brother will return tomorrow*'; **Nescivimus quot milites missurus esset** = '*We didn't know how many soldiers he would send.*' Any other tense of the subjunctive will be translated just as if it were the corresponding tense of the indicative. Examples: **Roga patrem quid in magno bello fecerit** = '*Ask father what he did in the great war*'; **Rogavi patrem cur nihil fecisset** = '*I asked father why he had done nothing*.' Here are a couple of examples from Caesar: a) **Ubi ex captivis cognovit quo in loco hostium copiae consedissent, ad hostes contendit** (B.G. V, 9) = '*When he discovered from prisoners in what place the enemy forces had taken up position, he marched towards the enemy*.' b) **Litteras Caesari remisit, quanto cum periculo legionem ex hibernis educturus esset** (B.G. V, 47). This example of a future subjunctive is a bit tricky because some verb like 'showing' – which Caesar didn't see fit to include since the sense was perfectly clear without it – has to be supplied in English. Translation: '*He sent back a despatch to Caesar, (showing/telling him) with how great danger/at how great risk he would lead out the legion from winter-quarters*.' If this passage were used in an O-Level Unseen, you can be sure that some Latin equivalent of 'showing', e.g., **quibus monstravit** = 'by which he showed', would be there in print. O-Level examiners recognise that neither Caesar nor any other Latin writer was writing for O-Level candidates.

There remains the double indirect question. This seldom occurs in O-Level Unseens, but you will find two or three examples of it in this book, and it must, therefore, be covered. Since you may not have met double direct questions, which are just as infrequent, it will be useful to take a look at these first. The rule for a double direct question is that it is introduced by **utrum** or **-ne** (words which are purely introductory and for which no equivalent will appear in English); that **an** = 'or', and that **an non** = 'or not'. Examples: **Utrum manebis/manebisne domi an exibis**? = '*Will you stay at home or go out?*'; **Utrum Caesar/Caesarne est in Italia an non**? = '*Is Caesar in Italy or not?*' A double indirect question differs only thus: a) the verb is in the subjunctive and b) 'or not' becomes **necne** instead of **an non**. Examples: **Rogavi utrum mansissent/mansissentne domi an exissent** = '*I asked whether they had stopped at home or gone out*'; **Dic mihi utrum velis/velisne ire necne** = '*Tell me whether you want to go or not*.' One further example – this time from Caesar – will suffice: **Perturbabantur copiasne adversus hostem ducere an castra defendere an fuga salutem petere praestaret** (B.G. IV, 14). Caesar is here using the verb **praestare** impersonally = 'to be best'.

Notice that this example is in fact a triple indirect question – a third possibility has been added to the more usual choice between alternatives. Translation: *'They were perplexed as to whether it was best to lead the troops against the enemy or to defend the camp or to seek safety by flight.'*

Unseen no. 9 contains three examples of indirect questions. To get three of them in one Unseen is most unusual – you will find many Unseens which contain none – but these three have not been deliberately introduced. The writer, Livy, from whom this Unseen is taken, happened to use three in quick succession. In fact, this Unseen is printed here exactly as it was when it was set at O Level, except for the omission of a three-word phrase in the ablative absolute construction. This Unseen contains, beside three indirect questions, three acc. and inf. constructions, two participles, one purpose clause, one indirect command. The meaning of the phrase **capita papaverum desecuit** is given you in the title. Unseen no. 10 contains, beside other constructions, one indirect question with its verb in a future tense and one double indirect question. Look at Appendix B to make sure that you don't mistranslate **fugaverint** (the last word in the Unseen) – as far too many did when this Unseen was set at O Level.

9 Without speaking a word, a father sends a message to his son at Gabii by cutting off poppy-heads

Sextus, filius Tarquini Superbi, regis Romanorum, Gabios abierat, simulans se hostem populi Romani esse. Gabini illum dono deorum sibi missum esse crediderunt; atque mox magnam potentiam apud eos habebat. tum unum ex suis Romam misit, ut cognosceret quid pater se facere vellet. rex nihil voce respondit, sed in hortum exiit. sequebatur eum fili nuntius. tum rex, ibi ambulans, summa papaverum capita gladio desecuit, nuntioque ut ad filium rediret imperavit. nuntius, Gabios regressus, rettulit filio quid vidisset. affirmavit regem, vel propter iram vel propter superbiam, nullum responsum dedisse. sed filius facile intellexit quid pater significaret; itaque principes Gabinorum, civitatis capita, interfecit.

10 A Persian army, having landed at Marathon, is defeated by the Athenians, who have been persuaded by Miltiades to march out and fight

Cum copiae Persarum ad Atticam pervenissent, castra posuerunt in campo qui Marathon appellatur abestque ab Athenis circiter decem milia passuum. in urbe Athenienses, qui nescierunt quid Persae facturi essent, disputabant utrum moenibus se defendere an hostibus obviam ire praestaret. unus dux, Miltiades, civibus persuasit ut quam celerrime cum hostibus confligerent. eius auctoritate impulsi, duces copias ex urbe eduxerunt et loco idoneo castra posuerunt. postero die aciem instruxerunt. dux Persarum, fretus[1] militum numero, putavit se statim dimicare debere. itaque exercitum in campum produxit proeliumque commisit. quo in proelio Athenienses tam acriter pugnaverunt ut primo impetu hostes fugaverint.

[1] **fretus** (with abl.), *relying on*

Ablative absolute

The construction traditionally called the Ablative Absolute is
unusual in giving more trouble to the translator from Latin to
English than it does to translators from English to Latin, who if they
wish, can dodge it altogether by using, instead, a **cum** -clause or
something similar. The word 'absolute' is mostly used in modern
English to mean 'complete', e.g., 'an absolute idiot'. In the phrase
'ablative absolute', it means 'detached', 'not dependent'. An ablative
absolute, therefore, is a 'detached' ablative. It consists of a noun or
pronoun in the ablative and a participle which is also in the ablative
and which agrees in number and gender with this noun or pronoun.
It is absolute because the phrase thus formed (noun/pronoun +
participle) is detached from, i.e., has no grammatical dependence
on, anything in the rest of the sentence in which it occurs. The best
approach to this construction is to take a look at the parallel
construction in English. Here, the parallel is a nominative absolute –
a construction not much used these days except in one or two
phrases. English examples: '*The beer having been delivered*, the party
could begin'; '*He having gone*, we all felt much happier.' (The use of
'he', a word with a distinguishable nominative in English, proves
that the construction is a *nominative* absolute. 'Him having gone'
would have been intelligible but ungrammatical.) Notice that each
italicised phrase is 'detached', i.e., is grammatically independent of
the rest of the sentence. Both phrases, though perfectly good
English, sound a bit pedantic these days; and normal usage would be
'since the beer had been delivered', 'when/after/since he had gone'.
On the other hand, the nominative phrase 'this being so' is much
commoner than 'since this is so'. But, apart from the odd phrase, the
nominative absolute certainly isn't used frequently in modern
English. In Latin, the ablative absolute, while it is never used with
future participles and only fairly frequently with present participles,
is used so frequently with perfect participles that, in the rest of the
Unseens in this book, you will meet it many times. We will start
with a very simple example: **Urbe capta**, **cives fugerunt**. Since
capio is an ordinary transitive verb, its perfect participle **captus** is,
as you have already seen in the section on Participles, passive in
meaning = '(having been) captured'. Therefore the simplest

translation of this example – and the one which is closest to the Latin – is: '*The city having been captured, the citizens fled.*' Translating thus, we are rendering a Latin ablative absolute by an English nominative absolute – an exact parallel to one that you have just seen: 'The beer having been delivered, the party could begin.' Just as, in present-day English, we would be more likely to say 'since the beer had been delivered', so we can say: 'Since the city had been captured, the citizens fled.' But the point to note is that the translation 'the city having been captured' is perfectly correct English. If, therefore, you translate all ablative absolutes which consist of noun/pronoun + a perfect participle of a transitive verb as '(something) having been (somethinged)', you cannot be marked wrong for doing so. On occasion, it will be inelegant English, but at O Level, examiners are looking for accuracy of translation, not elegance of style. Here are a couple of examples, taken from Caesar:

a) **Obsidibus traditis omnibusque armis ex oppido collatis, ab eo loco in fines Ambianorum pervenit** (B.G. II, 15) = '*Hostages having been handed over and all the arms having been collected from the town, he proceeded from that place to the territory of the Ambiani.*' Alternative translations of the ablative absolute phrases are 'after/when/since hostages had been handed over and all arms collected'. These alternatives are certainly more natural English, but 'hostages having been handed over' etc. is correct English and acceptable as such.

b) **Caesar paucos dies in eorum finibus moratus, omnibus vicis aedificiisque incensis, se in fines Ubiorum recepit** (B.G. IV, 19). This is a more complicated example, since beside the ablative absolute phrase (attached to nothing), we have also got the perfect participle of **moror**, a deponent and therefore active in meaning, attached to **Caesar**. A literal translation is: '*Caesar, having delayed for a few days in their territory, all the villages and buildings having been burned, withdrew into the territory of the Ubii.*' This inelegant translation would, at A Level, be penalised for its clumsiness. At O Level, it is acceptable, because it has one surpassing merit: it shows that the translator has completely understood the Latin. But you will naturally want to improve upon this clumsy English, and there are two obvious ways of doing this: either, 'Caesar withdrew after all the villages and buildings had been burned', or, since Caesar must have been the instigator of the action, 'Caesar withdrew after burning all the villages' etc. In any given instance, it is a matter for your own discretion whether, having seen the literal meaning (i.e., '*something* having been *somethinged*') you wish to improve upon a literal translation or to be content with showing the examiner that you have understood the Latin.

Ablative absolutes with a perfect participle deponent do not occur often. Remember, if you do meet such a one, that the participle will be active in meaning. Here is an example from Caesar: **Maximo coorto vento, fervefacta iacula in casas iacere coeperunt** (B.G. V, 43) = '*A very strong wind having sprung up, they began to throw incendiary javelins at the huts*.' Because, here, besiegers are taking advantage of a gale to set the huts alight in the besieged camp, you could write: 'since a very strong wind had sprung up'; but there is no need to do this. The literal translation is satisfactory in style as well as sense.

Present participles in the ablative absolute construction are not much of a problem for the translator. The phrase can usually be translated by a clause introduced by 'while' or 'since' followed by a verb in the imperfect indicative tense. E.g., **Hostibus fugientibus, Labienus equites produxit** = '*While/since the enemy were fleeing, Labienus brought forward his cavalry*.' (A clause introduced by 'while' or 'since' is better here than any attempt at a literal translation such as 'with the enemy fleeing' – which is in any case ungrammatical. The reason for using a clause is that, in modern English, the only present participle in regular use in a nominative absolute is 'being', e.g., 'this being so', 'other things being equal' etc.) In the example just given, either 'while' or 'since' will serve, but sometimes only 'while' will do. E.g., **Filia mecum in ripa ambulante, in flumen cecidi** = '*While my daughter was walking with me on the bank, I fell into the river*.' 'Since', here, would be nonsensical.

There is a type of phrase, in fairly common use in Latin, which has to be classified as an ablative absolute, though it contains no participle at all. Examples of this type of phrase are: **Caesare duce** = 'Caesar being leader', 'under the leadership of Caesar'; **nobis invitis** = 'we being unwilling', 'against our will'; **consulibus Pompeio et Crasso** = 'Pompeius and Crassus being consuls', 'in the consulship of Pompeius and Crassus'. Though the verb **sum** has no present participle = 'being', it is perhaps 'understood' in this type of phrase, which is included here in case you meet an example of it.

Unseen no. 11 contains four ablative absolutes and four other participles, besides one acc. and inf. and one indirect command. Appendix A will be helpful. Notice particularly that this Unseen provides examples of two (widely differing) meanings of **signum**. Avoid 'dart' as a translation for **telum**. (See Appendix A for this and for **signum**.) These days the word 'dart' suggests the saloon-bar rather than the battle-field. Appendix B will give you **iterum**, **aestus**, **paro**, **pareo**, **consisto**. You will get the meaning of **meridies** if you know what the 'English' abbreviations a.m. and p.m. really stand for. English derivatives will give you **fatigati** and **impendente**.

Unseen no. 12 contains three ablative absolutes as well as seven other participles.

1 Caesar, having defeated Pompey's troops in battle, goes on to attack his camp

Cum milites Pompeiani, in pugna superati, intra castrorum vallum se recepissent, Caesar, ratus[1] sibi occasionem datam esse, acie iterum instructa, cohortatus est suos ut beneficio fortunae uterentur castraque oppugnarent. hi, quamquam magno aestu erant fatigati (nam pugna ad meridiem erat perducta), ad omnem laborem animo parati, imperio paruerunt, atque, signo dato, ad vallum progressi sunt. sed milites Pompeiani, qui maximo periculo impendente ex acie refugerant, armis signisque militaribus abiectis iam cogitabant potius[2] de fuga quam[2] de castrorum defensione. neque ei qui in vallo constiterant multitudinem telorum diutius sustinere potuerunt, sed confecti vulneribus locum reliquerunt.

[1] **reor, reri, ratus sum**, *think*   [2] **potius . . . quam**, *rather than*

12 Romulus routs the Latins and dedicates a temple to Jupiter, giving the god the title Feretrius (god of spoils)

Latini, impetu in fines Romanorum facto, agros late vastabant. sed Romulus, qui paucis ante annis urbem Romanam condiderat, egressus cum exercitu vastantes facile fugavit eorumque regem in proelio interfectum spoliavit[1]. deinde, persecutus hostes, brevi tempore eorum urbem expugnavit. cum Romam redisset, ascendit in Capitolium, gerens arma regis occisi, ibique ea sub arborem sacram deposuit. simul, magna hominum multitudine adstante, dedicavit templum Iovi cognomenque addidit deo. 'Iupiter Feretri,' inquit, 'victor Romulus haec regis arma tibi fero, atque in his regionibus templum dedico, ad quod posteri, regibus ducibusque hostium interfectis, me imitantes optima spolia ferent.'

[1] **spoliare**, *strip (of arms, armour)*

Gerunds and gerundives

Participles, as you have seen, are verbal adjectives. Gerunds are
verbal nouns, i.e., they are nouns which imply action, and which,
like participles, are a part of a verb. Apart from a few irregulars, all
Latin verbs have a gerund. These gerunds are very easy to spot, and
the following endings cover the lot: **-andum** (1st conjugation),
endum (2nd and 3rd), **-iendum** (4th and hybrids of the **capio** type).
Gerunds are declined (in the singular only) just like any neuter noun
ending in **-um**, but they have no nominative (and of course no
vocative – we don't speak to gerunds). They are used in the
accusative only with a preposition in front of them. By going on to
say that you will translate them by using an English gerund, I am
myself at the same time providing you with two examples of an
English gerund, the words 'going' and 'using'. You may have seen
the English gerund described as 'a verbal noun in *-ing*'; and you can
readily see that it is a noun of sorts if, in the previous sentence, you
substitute for the gerund-phrase 'by using' an obvious noun-phrase
'by the use of'. We frequently use the English gerund in the
nominative or accusative, e.g., 'Swimming isn't difficult'; 'He
taught me swimming'. Latin, to put across similar ideas, uses the
present infinitive: **Natare non difficile est** (notice that the infinitive
thus used as verbal noun is neuter); **Me natare docuit**. This use of
the infinitive poses no problem for the translator, since the present
infinitive can equally be used in English: 'It's not difficult to swim';
'He taught me to swim.' The uses of the Latin gerund which the
translator has got to understand are as follows: a) with **ad** +
accusative to express purpose, e.g., **ad aquandum** = 'for the
purpose of getting water'; b) in the genitive (i) dependent on another
noun, e.g., **ars scribendi** = 'the art of writing' (ii) with **causa**
(which follows the gerund) = 'for the sake of', e.g., **praedandi**
causa = 'for the sake of looting' (iii) with one or two adjectives, of
which **cupidus** = 'desirous of/eager for' is the commonest, e.g.,
cupidus discendi = 'desirous of/eager for learning'; c) in the
ablative to express 'by', e.g., **cogitando** = 'by thinking'. (The very
infrequent use of the Latin gerund in the dative can safely be ignored
at O Level.) Once you have seen what a gerund is, you are not likely
to have any difficulty with any of these uses as such. Later examples

will show this, but first we must take a look at what, in text-book terminology, is called Gerundive Attraction.

This formidable phrase describes something which is a real difficulty for translators from English to Latin, but which is much less of a difficulty for translators from Latin to English. So far, we have looked at examples of the Latin gerund standing on its own, e.g., **aquandum**, **scribendi**, **cogitando**. But the second of the two English gerunds to which you were first introduced did in fact show the gerund followed by an object. The gerund + object phrase was: 'by using an English gerund'. The phrase looks harmless enough, but the snag is that a Latin gerund, unlike an English gerund, is seldom followed by a straightforward accusative-object. How, then, does Latin usually put across such ideas as 'by writing books', 'for the sake of helping your sister' (plainly gerund + object phrases in English)? The short answer is that gerundive attraction comes into play. The label isn't very informative in itself. What, in fact, happens is that Latin (i) replaces the gerund by the gerundive (which is an adjective) (ii) puts the noun which the phrase contains in the case in which the gerund would have been if it had been used (iii) makes the gerundive (which, as an adjective, has got to agree with something) agree with this noun. All this sounds alarmingly complicated. In practice, as you will soon see, it is far less complicated than it sounds. For the translator, the complication stems chiefly from the fact that there can be no corresponding construction in English (and therefore no literal translation) simply because, in English, there is no such thing as a gerundive. The Latin gerundive is a passive adjective, formed by replacing the **-um** ending of the gerund by adjectival endings **-us, -a, -um**. E.g., if **scribendum** is the gerund of **scribo** (as it is), the gerundive is **scribendus -a -um**. What does a gerundive mean? In the absence of an English gerundive, no precise answer is possible. Let us say that **scribendus** means something like 'to be written'. That will serve for the moment. We can now take the plunge and see how Latin expresses gerund + object phrases, i.e., how the rather complicated process already described works out in practice.

Take, as a first example, 'by writing books'. What one would expect to find in Latin is: **scribendo** (ablative of the gerund = 'by writing') **libros** (accusative-object). What one actually finds is **libris scribendis**. What, then, has happened? Just two things: (i) the noun

44

has been 'attracted' into the ablative because this is the case in which the gerund would have been if it had been used; (ii) the gerund has been replaced by the gerundive, which, being an adjective, naturally agrees with **libris**. The whole phrase, therefore, instead of just the gerund, has become ablative. Take the other example already mentioned: 'for the sake of helping your sister'. Again, one might have expected **iuvandi** (the genitive of the gerund) **causa** (following the gerund, as always, but making the gerund genitive) **tuam sororem** (accusative-object). Instead, because a gerund, if used, would have been genitive, we get the genitive **tuae sororis**; the gerundive replacing the gerund will have to agree with **sororis**; and the whole phrase will thus become genitive, apart of course from **causa**, which stays put, following the gerundive as it would have followed the gerund: **tuae sororis iuvandae causa**.

Such is gerundive attraction – 'gerundive' because the gerund is replaced by the gerundive, and 'attraction' because the noun is 'attracted' into the case in which the gerund would have been if it had been used. This traditional phrase is not very inspired labelling, but the label, as far as you are concerned, does not matter. What does matter is that, when translating an example of this combination of noun and gerundive, you remember the following points: (i) Look at the combination of noun and gerundive and decide what case they are in. (ii) Whatever the order of the Latin words, translate the gerundive first, naturally by an English gerund, in accordance with its case, i.e. with 'by', 'of' or whatever is required. (iii) Translate the noun (with which the gerundive agrees) just as though it were an accusative-object. Example: **Nobis datur occasio urbis prodendae** = 'An opportunity is given to us *of* betraying (**urbis prodendae** is clearly a genitive-phrase) the city' (the genitive **urbis** is translated as though it were an accusative-object). You have already seen that no literal translation of a noun + gerundive phrase is possible. One can say that the Latin way of expressing 'by writing books', **libris scribendis**, amounts to saying 'by books to-be-written'. It does amount to something like this, but, offered as a translation, 'by books to-be-written' is nonsensical. One more point: since the gerundive is a passive adjective, gerundive attraction only comes into play with verbs which have a passive – and in Latin this means verbs which take an accusative-object. It does not come into play with verbs followed by a dative. Instead, the gerund is

45

retained, followed of course by a dative. E.g., **persuadendo militibus** = 'by persuading the troops'. Finally, take a look at a sentence from Caesar, which, beside containing a gerund and gerundives, will also give you a refresher on result-clauses:

Temporis tanta fuit exiguitas hostiumque tam paratus ad dimicandum animus ut non modo ad insignia accommodanda sed etiam ad galeas induendas tempus defuerit (B.G. II, 21) = '*The shortage of time was so great and the spirit of the enemy so ready for (the purpose of) fighting that not only was time lacking for (the purpose of) fixing on badges but also for (the purpose of) putting on helmets.*' (Notice that here, as often, 'for' by itself is a sufficient translation for this type of **ad** expressing purpose.) **Ad dimicandum** is a straightforward gerund without an object. **Ad insignia accommodanda** and **ad galeas induendas** are examples of gerundive attraction = (literally) 'for badges to-be-fixed on', and 'for helmets to-be-put on'. Unseen no. 13 contains three straightforward gerunds and three examples of gerundive attraction. It also contains one acc. and inf., one purpose-clause, two indirect commands, one ablative absolute, and four participles. This is not a 'military' passage, and Appendix A will help you only with **proficiscor**, **regredior**, **consisto**, **incolumis**. Appendix B will give you **aurum**, **parco**, **vita**, **solus**. **Cantare**, which in various forms occurs three times and is important to the general understanding of the passage, is a word which you should know. If you don't, the English word 'chant' is a clue but is not precise enough in itself. Unseen no. 14 contains one example of a gerund and three examples of gerundive attraction.

13 Arion is saved from death by a dolphin

Arion, clarissimus poeta, profectus est Corintho ad Siciliam, ut ibi cantando divitias sibi compararet. paucis post mensibus, adeptus[1] magnas divitias hoc faciendo, Corinthum regredi cupiebat. conscendit igitur navem quam suo auro oneraverat. sed cum in medio mari esset, cognovit nautas, cupidos auri abripiendi[2], sibi mortem machinari[3]. postquam frustra eos oravit ut sibi parcerent, rogavit ut in exitu vitae cantare sibi liceret. itaque indutus[4] veste splendida constitit solus in puppi[5], carminis supremi cantandi causa. tum, carmine finito, captus[6] moriendi cupidine, in mare desiluit. sed delphinus, dulci voce hominis delectatus, eum in tergo excepit, et, celeriter natando, brevi tempore incolumem ad litus portavit.

[1] **adipiscor, -i, adeptus sum**, *obtain*   [2] **abripere**, *snatch away*
[3] **machinari**, *to plot*   [4] **indutus**, *clothed*
[5] **puppis**, *stern (of a ship)*   [6] **captus**, *captivated*

14 Arriving at the river Oxus, Alexander transports his men with the aid of skins stuffed with straw

Alexander contendendo celeriter ad flumen Oxum cum paucis militibus fere solis occasu pervenit atque ibi castra posuit. sed magna pars exercitus non potuerat reliquos consequi. itaque in alto monte ignes fieri rex iussit. hoc signo dando effecit ut[1] milites qui sequebantur cognoscerent se castris appropinquare. ipse in via constitit neque a statione discessit antequam omne agmen praeterierat. postero die consilium fluminis transeundi iniit. neque enim naves habebat, nec ponte aedificando transire potuit quia ripae fluminis arboribus carebant[2]. itaque militibus imperavit ut flumen transnatarent, utentes utribus stramento refertis. milites hoc faciendo flumen transierunt; et illi qui primum ad ulteriorem ripam pervenerant ceteros exspectabant, parati ad hostes repellendos.

[1] **efficere ut**, *to bring it about that*   [2] **carere** + abl., *to lack*

Gerundives expressing necessity

In Latin, there are various ways of expressing the general idea of necessity which in English we convey by means of the verbs 'must', 'ought', and the use of 'have to' in the sense of something 'having to be done'. **Debeo** + present infinitive, the impersonal verb **oportet** + accusative and present infinitive, **necesse est** + dative and present infinitive – any of these can be used, but by far the most frequent way of expressing necessity is by the use of the gerundive. While tracking through the complications of gerundive attraction, you have in fact come across something which is a useful lead-in to the use of the gerundive as a 'necessity-word'. Apart from learning (if you did not already know) that the gerundive is a passive adjective, you saw that the nearest that one can get to a literal translation of such a phrase as **libris scribendis** is 'by books to-be-written'. Although the uses of the gerundive in gerundive attraction and as a 'necessity-word' are distinct, it is not difficult to see how **libri scribendi sunt** ('books are to-be-written') is the usual Latin way of saying 'books must be written'. Here are further simple examples: **Pons aedificandus erit** = '*A bridge will have to be built*'; **Urbs defendenda erat** = '*The city had to be defended*'; **Scis urbem defendendam esse** = '*You know that the city must be defended*'; **Nuntius Caesari mittendus est** = '*A messenger must be sent by Caesar.*' As you can see, Latin uses with the gerundive whatever part of **sum** the sense requires, including, of course, an infinitive, since, as one of our examples illustrates, a gerundive can be part of an acc. and inf. construction. Notice that, in the last of these examples, 'by Caesar' is not **a Caesare** but **Caesari**, i.e. the dative. This is because, with gerundives used as 'necessity-words', the agent, i.e. the person by whom the action, whatever it is, has to be done, is in the dative – a point which you must remember when translating. This use of the dative is not really difficult to understand: in the example just used, Caesar is the man *for* whom the necessity exists. We can now look at an example from Caesar himself in which he uses a string of gerundives and puts himself in the dative as being the man by whom the various things had to be done: **Caesari omnia uno tempore erant agenda: vexillum proponendum, signum tuba dandum, ab opere revocandi milites, acies instruenda, milites cohortandi** (B.G.

II, 20). Translation: '*Everything had to be done at once by Caesar: the flag (had to be) hoisted: the signal (had to be) given by a trumpet, the soldiers (had to be) recalled from their work, the battle-line (had to be) drawn up, the soldiers (had to be) encouraged*.' Notice that, just as, in English, 'had to be' does not need to be repeated each time, so Caesar does not repeat **erat/erant** with each gerundive. Notice, too, that the sixth word in this extract from Caesar is **agenda**. This word, which by itself = 'things to be done', is used freely in English by countless people who are unaware of the existence of Latin gerundives, as are other gerundives such as 'propaganda' = 'things/opinions to be spread further', 'referendum' = 'a thing to be referred'. Unawareness leads to error. Politicians and journalists, perhaps with a hazy memory of Latin, use 'referenda' as the plural of 'referendum'. They are wrong. 'Referenda', as you will readily see, = 'things to be referred', whereas the meaning they want is 'a thing (singular) to be referred' to two or more lots of people, and the word they should use is 'referendums'.

Since the gerundive is a passive adjective, all Latin clauses/ sentences in which it is used as a 'necessity-word' are automatically in the passive, provided that the verb is transitive. In English, we have a preference for verbs in the active, where this is possible. Instead of saying 'everything had to be done by Caesar', we should be more likely to say 'Caesar had to do everything.' Since either translation is equally correct, there is no snag here for the translators from Latin to English, who can keep to the passive, or, if they think it sounds better, swing the clause/sentence round into the active.

Although intransitive verbs have no passive as such, Latin still uses a gerundive of these verbs, but uses it in a different way. This gerundive is used impersonally in the nominative, and, because it is impersonal, it has the neuter ending **-um**. Examples: **Eundum est tibi** = 'There must be a going by you' = 'you must go'; **Omnibus moriendum est** = 'There must be a dying by all' = 'All must die.' As you have seen, Latin verbs which are followed by a dative are intransitive, though they have a transitive meaning in English. Naturally Latin uses these, too, with an impersonal gerundive. Taking as an example **persuadeo**, which, since it takes a dative, is an intransitive verb in Latin (though 'persuade' is a transitive verb in English), we get: **Ei a te non persuadendum est** = 'There must not be a persuading him by you' = 'You ought not to persuade him.'

Here, **a te** replaces the usual agent-dative with gerundives, as two datives (**ei** already being present after **persuadendum est**) would have been confusing.

Unseen no. 15 contains three gerundives of necessity – one with a transitive verb, one with an intransitive verb, and one in the acc. and inf. construction. It also contains two purpose-clauses. Unseen no. 16 contains two gerundives of necessity, both of them in the acc. and inf. construction.

Conditional clauses

You will meet Conditional Clauses now and again in O-Level Unseens. If the verbs in these clauses are in the indicative, they should give you no trouble, since Latin indicatives will be translated by the corresponding English indicatives – except when Latin is using future indicative tenses. You have to remember that, with future tenses, the idiom of Latin differs from that of English, and that a Latin future or future perfect in the '**si** – clause' has to be translated by an English present. Example: **Si cras Romam iveris/ibis, meum fratrem videbis** = '*If you go to Rome tomorrow, you will see my brother*.' In the English, 'go' is not a true present, since it is plainly standing for 'will go', but in translation you will have to accept our illogical English idiom. Remember that, besides **si**, a conditional clause can be introduced by **nisi** = 'unless', 'if . . . not'. Remember, too, that **quis** and **quid**, when they follow **si**, mean 'anyone', 'anything'.

The types of conditional in which Latin uses the subjunctive will give you no difficulty, provided that you have memorised what each type means. Here is a brief summary:

Present Subjunctive: **Si hoc dicas, erres** = '*If you were to say this, you would be wrong*.' This conditional looks to the future, though more vaguely than a conditional using future indicatives, and, as the text books put it, it is 'capable of fulfilment'.

Imperfect Subjunctive: **Si Caesar viveret, veterrimus esset** = '*If Caesar were alive, he would be very old*.' This conditional refers to present time and it is 'incapable of fulfilment' (Caesar, at least in the obvious sense of the word, is not alive).

Pluperfect Subjunctive: **Si hoc dixisses, erravisses** = '*If you had said this, you would have been wrong*.' This conditional refers to past time and it is 'incapable of fulfilment' (you did not say this).

For no particular reason, this last-mentioned type of conditional seems to occur more frequently than any other in O-Level Unseens. Unseen no. 15 contains two conditionals, and no. 16 contains one.

15 Milo, while making a journey, is ambushed by Clodius

Illo die, iter Miloni faciendum erat. quod cum Clodius cognovisset, amicis 'Miloni' inquit 'moriendum est hodie. si properabimus, eum consequemur[1]. ipse igitur una cum compluribus amicis Roma profectus est, ut ante suum fundum[2] Miloni insidias faceret. occurrit ei ante fundum hora undecima. statim multi cum telis in Milonem impetum fecerunt. cum is de raeda[3] desiluisset gladiumque eduxisset, illi qui cum Clodio erant rem celeriter conficiendam esse senserunt. itaque alii recurrerunt ad raedam ut a tergo Milonem adorirentur, alii caedere incipiunt[4] eius servos, qui post erant atque domino succurrere conabantur. ac vero Milo ipse occisus esset, nisi acri animo se defendisset.

[1] **consequi**, *catch up with*   [2] **fundus**, *farm*
[3] **raeda**, *carriage*   [4] **incipere**, *begin*

16 King Iugurtha attempts to seize by force the kingdom of Adherbal, and a battle takes place near Cirta

Adherbal, cum intellexisset regnum suum aut relinquendum esse aut armis retinendum, copias parat. mox haud longe a mari prope Cirtam oppidum exercitus Adherbalis Iugurthaeque instructi sunt. sed, quia iam vesper erat, proelium non commissum est. sed media nocte milites Iugurthae signo dato castra hostium invadunt, semisomnosque homines facile fugant. Adherbal cum paucis equitibus Cirtam profugit, et nisi multitudo civium Romanorum ibi fuisset, qui Iugurthae copias moenibus prohibuerunt, uno die inter duos reges bellum coeptum atque confectum esset. Iugurtha igitur oppidum obsedit et machinis omnium generum expugnare conatus est.

Verbs of fearing

The three Latin verbs meaning 'fear/am afraid' which you are likely to meet are **timeo**, **vereor**, **metuo**. All three can be followed by a present infinitive, as in English: **Timet ire** = '*He is afraid to go*.' But, in O-Level Unseens, you are far more likely to find them followed by a clause, as in English: 'I am afraid that he has gone.' In Latin, such clauses are introduced by **ne** and have their verb in the subjunctive. As examples will show, **ne** after a fearing-verb means 'that' or 'lest' (*never* 'that . . . not' – a meaning of **ne** which is confined to purpose clauses). We must now see what tenses of the subjunctive are used and what they mean. Obviously a fear can be about the present, the future, or the past. The way in which Latin handles these three possibilities is best seen in examples. If the fearing-verb is in a primary tense (i.e. present, present-perfect or future), Latin expresses a fear about the present or future by the present subjunctive (the so-called future subjunctive is not used in this construction): **Timeo ne sero adveniat** = '*I fear/am afraid that he may/will arrive/is arriving too late*.' If the fearing-verb is in a historic tense (i.e., imperfect, perfect, pluperfect), the imperfect subjunctive is used: **Veritus sum ne sero adveniret** = '*I feared/was afraid that he might/would arrive/was arriving too late*.' A fear about the past gives no trouble at all, since either a perfect (in primary time) or a pluperfect (in historic time) subjunctive is used, to be translated by the corresponding indicative tenses in English: **Metuo ne non advenerit** = '*I am afraid that he hasn't arrived/didn't arrive*' (notice that, if the **ne**-clause is negatived, this is done by inserting **non** or whatever negative is required); **Veriti ne nuntius ad Caesarem non advenisset, ad eruptionem faciendam nos paravimus** = '*Fearing that the messenger hadn't reached Caesar, we got ourselves ready for making a break-out*.' Be on the look-out for the perfect participle of **vereor** which introduces the **ne**-clause here. It occurs quite frequently, and of course strictly means 'having feared', but 'fearing' is the natural English translation. If you wish, you can translate **ne** after a fearing-verb by 'lest' – a common enough practice in English at one time. These days, 'lest' has a rather old-fashioned sound, but the use of it after a fearing-verb is never wrong. One last point: **terreo** (= 'frighten'), although not a fearing-verb as such, can be followed by a similar **ne**-clause when it is used in the passive: **Territi ne urbs caperetur, ad portam cucurrerunt** = '*Frightened that the city might be captured, they ran to the gate*.'

Unseen no. 17 contains two examples of a fearing-verb followed by a clause introduced by **ne**. No. 18 contains one – and it also contains that comparative rarity, a double indirect question.

Unseen no. 18 and all subsequent Unseens are exactly as they appeared when set for O Level. In no. 17, just one sentence has been altered. In line 6, the original version was: **sed discessum suum ab Hannibale sentiri noluit**. In order to give you practice with a **ne**-clause after a fearing-verb, I have altered this to what is in fact a slightly harder version: **sed metuebat ne discessus suus ab Hannibale sentiretur**. In working the rest of the Unseens, i.e., nos. 19–36, you are on your own, apart from a foot-note or two, as far as this book is concerned. This, therefore, is the last opportunity for giving advice, and it is best utilised by pointing out to you – so that you yourself may guard against them – typical mistakes which candidates made in an actual Unseen when it was worked in the O-Level examination. Unseen no. 17 will serve as well as any other. It was set in the O-Level examination, Summer 1974. This Unseen contains a useful mixture of constructions – useful for testing a candidate's knowledge and discernment. These are: three acc. and inf., one purpose-clause, one indirect command (involving two verbs), one fearing-verb + **ne** (to which I have added another which was not in the original version), three participles, two of which are deponents. As is to be expected at this stage, there is nothing, on the construction side, which you have not covered in this book. We can, therefore, leave constructions out of it, though naturally the weaker candidates bungled any or all of them in various ways. It is better to see how the marks dribbled away because of other mistakes. The Unseen contains three adjectives in the superlative degree. These, particularly **proxima**, were often translated as positives. Surprisingly, **at** (line 2) was not translated at all by at least 30% of the candidates, and some 20% of those who noticed it mistranslated it as 'and'. The fact that the words **Alpes transisse** (line 3) are side by side was sufficient to produce a fair crop of 'Alps were crossed'. **Iungerentur** (line 5) and **adiunxit** (line 12) both gave trouble as vocabulary; but in the first half of the Unseen the phrase which defeated a great number of candidates was **obviam iret** (lines 5/6).

Legatis (line 8) is a word which, as you know, has two distinct meanings. Many candidates chose the wrong one, even though, in this context, it made no sense at all. **Auderet** (line 10) was translated by far too many as if it were a part of **audio**. This, of course, was a predictable error. Much less predictable was the number of candidates who threw away a mark by translating **in Umbriam** (line 11) as though it were 'in Umbria'. (One would expect even the weakest candidates to know the difference in meaning between **in** + acc. and **in** + abl.) There was one really difficult clause in this Unseen. Before looking at this, let us see how you can protect yourself against the errors so far mentioned and other errors which were also made, though less frequently. **Obviam ire** is in Appendix A. (It is also given in the title.) Appendix A contains **castra** and **castra pono**, **cognosco**, **transeo**, **deleo**, **copiae**, **proficiscor**, **discessus** (also given in the title), **legatus**, **servo**, **oppugno**, **pauci**, **progredior**, **educo**, **supero**. Appendix B contains **at** and **et**, **audio** and **audeo**, **facies** and **facile**, **constituo** and **consisto**. In *How to Tackle an Unseen*, you were shown how to get the meaning of **iungerentur** and **adiunxit** from an English derivative. English derivatives will also help you to get the meanings of **arderent**, **suspicatus**, **duplicatis**. Above all, advice already given you will, if you follow it, enable you to translate correctly what proved to be the one really difficult clause in the Unseen. This difficult clause is: **et eadem facies castrorum servaretur** (line 9). Only the better or (for a reason which we shall see in a minute) the more observant candidates got it completely right. In contrast with these, I quote this example of a translation which is about as bad as it could be: 'and those easily were the savers of the camp'. **Facies** has been confused with **facile**; **eadem** has been a) mistranslated and b) taken as a masculine plural, whereas, if it is a plural at all, it has got to be neuter; **servaretur**, which is clearly singular, has been taken as a plural to match up with the mistranslation 'those', and in any case has itself been mistranslated; 'of the camp' is correct. The candidate who wrote this rubbish got quite a lot of the rest of the Unseen right, including the clause **ut . . . arderent** which immediately precedes the clause that he/she butchered. One thing is certain: this sudden descent into writing rubbish could have been avoided if this candidate had received, and remembered, a piece of advice which I gave you at the very beginning of *How to Tackle an Unseen*. You were there advised to 'read the English title carefully'. When I was setting this Unseen, I realised that the clause **et eadem . . . servaretur** was likely to be found difficult. I therefore incorporated in the English title a very substantial clue: 'that the outward appearance of his camp remained the same'. This clue is so substantial as to be almost a translation, yet it was totally ignored by this particular candidate and by a good many others as well. In this book, you have been given advice on how to avail yourself of any help given, and on a great deal else as well. It is for you to use that advice, while at the same time remembering that, for anyone facing an examination in Latin, at O Level or any other level, there is no substitute for knowledge of Latin. The advice that you have been given is to enable you to make the best use of your knowledge.

17 Nero, setting out with part of his army to confront Hasdrubal, conceals his departure from Hannibal by ensuring that the outward appearance of his camp remained the same

Consul Claudius Nero castra posuerat proxima castris Hannibalis, qui in Apulia manebat. at cum cognovisset Hasdrubalem, fratrem Hannibalis, Alpes transisse, maximi momenti[1] esse putabat copias eius delere antequam Hannibali iungerentur. proficisci igitur constituit ut Hasdrubali obviam iret; sed metuebat ne discessus suus ab Hannibale sentiretur. itaque decem milia fortissimorum militum elegit imperavitque legatis quos relinquebat ut totidem[2] ignes arderent et eadem facies castrorum servaretur. timuit enim ne Hannibal, suspicatus se falli, auderet oppugnare eos qui pauci in castris relicti essent. tum, progressus in Umbriam, se adiunxit collegae Livio, qui Roma exercitum eduxerat. his duplicatis copiis Nero Hasdrubalem facile superavit.

[1] **momentum**, *importance*   [2] **totidem**, *just as many*

8 Coriolanus, having deserted to the Volsci, is approached by his wife and mother

Coriolanus, qui fuerat dux Romanus, fugit ad Volscos, hostes Romanorum, atque iam contra patriam pugnabat. matronae Romanae, veritae ne Roma a Coriolano oppugnaretur, ad Veturiam eius matrem Volumniamque uxorem venerunt. persuaserunt eis ut in castra hostium secum irent, et, quoniam armis urbem defendere non possent, precibus[1] lacrimisque conservarent. ubi ad castra ventum est, Coriolano nuntiatum est adesse ingens mulierum agmen. tum amicus quidam, qui illas cognoverat, 'Nisi me oculi decipiunt', inquit, 'mater tua uxorque adsunt.' Coriolanus a sua sede surrexit ut matri complexum[2] daret. sed illa, in iram ex precibus versa, 'Cupio scire', inquit, 'priusquam complexum accipio, utrum ad hostem an ad filium venerim.'

[1] **preces**, *prayers* [2] **complexus**, *an embrace*

19 When his troops are exhausted by thirst, Alexander refuses to drink a cup of water which was not intended for him

Exercitus Alexandri, cum per loca aridissima iter faceret, siti oppressus est. ac rex ipse, anxius in tanto periculo, nesciebat quid faciendum esset. tum duo milites ex paucis qui ad locum castris capiendum praecesserant ad reliquos redierunt, aquam portantes ut filiis suis, qui sitim pati non poterant, succurrerent. qui cum regem vidissent, alter ex eis implevit aqua poculum, quod regi obtulit. ille poculum accepit sed statim rogavit ad quos aquam portarent. atque cum cognovisset illos ad filios portare, poculum reddidit. 'nec solus bibere sustineo', inquit, 'nec possum dividere tam parvum inter omnes. vos currite et filiis vestris id quod propter illos attulistis date.'

20 By illustrating two ways of pulling out a horse's tail, Sertorius shows that the Roman contingents must be attacked one by one

Sertorius, dum contra Romanos in Hispania pugnat, cognovit suum exercitum parvum non posse totas Romanorum copias simul superare. milites tamen imprudentes pugnam statim poscebant. Sertorius, ut eos in sententiam suam verteret, in conspectum eorum duos adduxit equos, alterum validum, alterum debilem[1]. tum elegit duos iuvenes, alterum robustum, alterum gracilem[2]. ac iuvenem robustum iussit equi debilis[1] totam caudam abrumpere, gracilem[2] autem iussit caudam equi validi per singulos pilos[3] extrahere. tum hic gracilis[2] facile fecit quod imperatum est, ille robustus sine effectu laborabat. deinde 'naturam', inquit militibus Sertorius, 'Romanarum copiarum vobis ostendi per hoc exemplum. insuperabiles erunt si totas oppugnabimus. si singulas temptabimus, facile superabimus.'

[1] **debilis**, *weak*   [2] **gracilis**, *thin*, *slender*   [3] **pilus**, *hair*

1 **The Spartan king Agesilaus, beginning an attack upon the Persian king, finds that Tissaphernes, one of the Persian governors, is a man who does not keep his word**

Agesilaus civibus persuasit ut bellum contra regem Persarum facerent. nam fama erat hunc regem parare copias quas in Graeciam mitteret. Agesilaus tam celeriter cum exercitu contendit, ut in Asiam pervenerit priusquam regis praefecti scirent eum profectum esse. id cum cognovisset Tissaphernes, qui tum inter praefectos summum imperium habebat, indutias[1] ab Agesilao petivit, simulans se pacem et amicitiam velle. uterque iuravit se indutias conservaturum esse. sed quamquam Agesilaus fidem servavit, Tissaphernes nihil aliud quam bellum comparavit. quod cum Agesilaus sensisset, dixit Tissaphernem mala fide sua et homines et deos offensurum esse. quibus verbis auditis milites putaverunt se praefectum perfidiosum facile victuros esse.

[1] **indutiae**, *truce*

2 **A serpent, seen in a dream, reveals the whereabouts of a root which heals wounds inflicted by a poisoned missile**

Ptolemaeus, amicus regis Alexandri, in proelio telo venenato vulneratus erat. dum eo vulnere summo cum dolore moritur, Alexander sedens prope eius lectum somno superatus est. tum in somnio apparuit ei serpens, qui radiculam in ore ferebat. atque regem alloquens serpens affirmavit vim radiculae tantam esse ut Ptolemaeum facile sanare posset. simul regi dixit quo in loco illa radicula inveniretur (neque is locus longe aberat). rex, cum e somno surrexisset, amicis somnium narravit emisitque statim milites qui illam radiculam quaererent. qua inventa, non modo Ptolemaeus sanatus est, sed etiam multi milites qui eodem genere teli erant vulnerati.

23 Alexander and his Macedonians are attacked by a people who use chariots linked together

Alexander ad magnam urbem pervenit, cuius incolae ad pugnandum egressi sunt, vehiculis inter se iunctis. hi barbari, hastis armati, transiliebant[1] ex alio in aliud vehiculum cum suis succurrere vellent. ac primo hoc novum genus pugnae Macedones terruit, cum telis undique coniectis vulnerarentur. postea autem, vehiculis ab utroque latere simul oppugnatis, barbaros interficere coeperunt. et Alexander iussit vincula quibus vehicula iuncta erant incidi[2], quo* facilius singula circumvenirentur. itaque hostes, octo milibus suorum amissis, in oppidum refugerunt. postero die, scalis[3] admotis, muri a Macedonibus occupati sunt. pauci ex hostibus in oppida proxima fugerunt intuleruntque magnum terrorem affirmantes exercitum qui vinci non posset appropinquare.

[1] **transilire**, *leap across*   [2] **incidere**, *cut through*
[3] **scala**, *ladder*
*In a purpose clause containing a comparative adjective or adverb, **quo** takes the place of **ut**.

24 A similarity between the name of king Perses and the name of a dog provides Paulus with a good omen

Q. Cicero, qui credebat verba humana res futuras praedicere posse, talis ominis dat hoc exemplum: L. Paulus consul creatus est ad conficiendum bellum quod cum rege Perse Romani gerebant; ea ipsa die domum ad vesperum rediit atque osculans filiam suam Tertiam sensit eam tristissimam esse. 'Quid est', inquit, 'mea Tertia? Cur tristis es?' 'Mi pater,' inquit, 'Persa periit.' eis verbis puella significavit canem suum eo nomine mortuum esse. sed Paulus, puellam complexus[1], 'accipio', inquit, 'mea filia, omen.' nam, audito canis mortui nomine, pro certo habuit regem Persen in bello moriturum esse. neque omen vanum erat; nam Paulus copias hostium fugavit atque regem ipsum necavit.

[1] **complector, -i, complexus sum**, *embrace*

60

5 **The Lacedaemonian leader, Pausanias, victor over the Persians at Plataea, dies a shameful death, to which his own mother makes her contribution**

Pausanias Persas superaverat apud Plataeam proelio illustrissimo. sed mox Lacedaemonii cognoverunt eum habere consilia patriae inimica. itaque Spartam revocatus est, quod cives putaverunt facilius eum in urbe comprehendi posse. sed Pausanias, cum in urbem intraturus esset, intellexit ex vultu civis cuiusdam, qui eum admonere cupiebat, se in maximum periculum adductum esse. confugit igitur in templum Minervae. hinc ne exire posset, Lacedaemonii statim templi portas obstruxerunt tectumque demoliti sunt, quo celerius sub caelo periret. dicitur eo tempore mater Pausaniae, postquam de scelere filii comperit, primos ad eum claudendum lapides ad templi introitum attulisse. tali modo Pausanias magnam belli gloriam turpi morte maculavit[1].

[1] **maculare**, *to stain*

6 **The citizens of Tyre, a city separated from the mainland by a narrow strait, are prepared to welcome Alexander as an ally, but refuse to allow him within their walls**

Urbs Tyrus, in qua est templum Herculis clarissimum, a continenti dividitur freto angusto. cum urbi appropinquaret rex Alexander, Tyrii societatem eius accipere volebant. coronam igitur auream multaque alia dona legati ad regem portaverunt. Alexander dona accepit benigneque legatos allocutus indicavit se velle urbem intrare ut Herculi sacrificaret. sed Tyrii responderunt esse alterum templum Herculis extra urbem; ibi regem deo sacrificare posse. tum rex iram non tenuit. 'Vos,' inquit 'quod insulam incolitis, meum pedestrem exercitum spernitis, sed brevi tempore ostendam in continenti vos habitare. vestram urbem enim aut intrabo aut oppugnabo.'

27 An African tribe, the Austoriani, pillage the Lepcitani, who appeal in vain to the Romans for help

Austoriani, qui barbari rapinis et caedibus vivere
solebant, impetu in Lepcitanorum fines facto, agros late
vastaverunt, agricolas interfecerunt, domos incenderunt.
perterriti hac subita clade, Lepcitani auxilium imploraverunt
Romani ducis qui tum provinciae Africae praeerat. qui cum
venisset, magnas copias ducens, affirmavit se castra non
moturum esse ad barbaros oppugnandos, nisi Lepcitani
abundantem commeatum et camelorum quattuor milia sibi
dedissent. stupefacti hoc responso, miseri cives negaverunt se
posse post tot vastationes et incendia praebere tantam copiam
frumenti et camelorum. itaque Romanus, ibi moratus
quadraginta dies ut eos falsa spe deluderet, discessit nullo
auxilio dato.

28 By means of a trench drawn in front of the town of Panormus, Metellus is enabled to defeat Hasdrubal and to capture his elephants

L. Metellus consul bellum adversus Hasdrubalem in
Sicilia gerebat. sed turbatus ob ingentem eius exercitum et
ducentos elephantos, simulato metu, intra Panormum copias
tenuit fossamque ingentis magnitudinis ante se duxit.
conspecto deinde exercitu Hasdrubalis, qui in prima acie suos
elephantos habebat, Metellus suis militibus imperavit ut tela in
beluas[1] iacerent statimque se intra munitiones reciperent. ea
audacia irati, rectores elephantorum in ipsam fossam
elephantos egerunt. quo cum primum inlati essent, alii
multitudine telorum oppressi sunt, alii retro in suos acti totam
aciem turbaverunt. tum Metellus, qui hanc occasionem
exspectabat, toto cum exercitu erupit et hostes a latere
aggressus superavit ipsisque elephantis potitus est.

[1] **belua**, *beast*

9 The Romans attacking Syracuse are thwarted by the devices of Archimedes

Syracusae terra marique a Romanis obsideri coeptae sunt; et urbs brevi tempore capta esset, nisi unus homo illo tempore Syracusis fuisset. Archimedes is erat, non modo unicus spectator caeli stellarumque sed etiam admirabilis inventor bellicorum tormentorum[1]. cum Romani sexaginta naves in portum Syracusarum adduxissent, Archimedes tormenta varia in muris disposuit. in eas naves quae procul erant saxa ingentis ponderis emittebat; propiores levioribus telis oppugnabat. Romani igitur, multis navibus amissis, urbem terra aggressi sunt. sed iterum Archimedis arte urbs est defensa. quae cum in colle aedificata esset, saxa tormentis emissa in hostes gravissime incidebant multosque interficiebant. itaque Romani oppugnatione desistere coacti sunt.

[1] **tormenta** (n.pl.), *artillery*

10 Catulus escapes from the Cimbri by pretending to pitch camp

Catulus, dux Romanus, a Cimbris pulsus erat. atque cum unam spem salutis haberet si transisset flumen, cuius ripas hostes tenebant, in summo monte copias ostendit, tamquam[1] ibi castra positurus. tum imperavit suis ne sarcinas[2] solverent aut onera deponerent aut ab ordinibus discederent. et quo facilius hostibus persuaderet se manere constituisse, pauca tabernacula in conspectu erigi iussit ignesque fieri et quosdam exire ut ligna[3] colligerent. quibus visis, Cimbri Catulum vere castra posuisse existimantes ipsi castris locum delegerunt. tum, dispersi in proximos agros ad petenda ea quae necessaria erant, occasionem Catulo dederunt non solum flumen transeundi sed etiam castra eorum oppugnandi.

[1] **tamquam**, *as if*   [2] **sarcina**, *a pack*   [3] **ligna** (n.pl.), *firewood*

31 King Alexander, on his way to the Far East, is alarmed by the behaviour of his soldiers

Rex Alexander in urbe quadam a Graecis condita complures dies manebat, dum frumentum undique confertur. itaque rumor per exercitum perlatus est, regem, contentum eis rebus quas gessisset, in Macedoniam redire statuisse. statim milites in tabernacula currunt et itineri impedimenta parant. crederes signum iam datum esse ut castra moverent. celeriter regi nuntiatum est quid facerent milites. ille, qui per Indiam atque ultimas Orientis partes iter facere constituerat, praefectos copiarum convocavit. lacrimans questus est se e summae gloriae spe revocari, si milites domum reverti iam cuperent. tum vero praefecti, permoti eius lacrimis, promittunt se militibus persuasuros esse ut ad Orientem proficiscerentur.

32 King Agesilaus prevents some young men from deserting Sparta when the Thebans are attacking it

Cum Thebani Spartam, quod oppidum sine muris erat, oppugnarent, rex Agesilaus sua prudentia civitatem conservavit. nam cum quidam adulescentes, perterriti hostium adventu, ad Thebanos transfugere vellent et, ex urbe egressi, collem proximum occupavissent, Agesilaus statim intellexit fore maximo periculo si cives cognovissent illos ad hostes transfugere conari. itaque ad collem venit cum militibus, atque consilium fortitudinemque adulescentium laudavit quod* locum ad urbem defendendam idoneum cepissent*. hac falsa laudatione rex adulescentes ad fidem revocavit, et adiunctis suis militibus locum tutum reliquit. nam adulescentes, deterriti adventu militum qui consilium transfugiendi ignorabant, a colle discedere non ausi sunt.

*cepissent is subjunctive because the reason is a suggested one (quod = *on the ground that*)

33 The shepherd Gyges becomes king of Lydia by using a magic ring which he found in a cave

De Gyge Plato, ille vir sapientissimus, narrat hanc fabulam. olim Gyges, qui erat pastor regis Lydiae, forte descendit in antrum magnum quod in terra factum erat, et in latere eius antri portam conspexit. qua aperta, vidit corpus hominis mortui magnitudine singulari anulumque aureum in digito. cum anulum detraxisset et in suo digito posuisset, tum in pastorum concilium intravit. ibi, cum palam[1] eius anuli ad palmam verterat, a nullo videbatur, sed ipse omnia videbat. rursus videbatur cum in locum anulum inverterat. itaque hac opportunitate usus regem dominum interfecit, nec in hoc scelere eum quisquam potuit videre. sic statim anuli beneficio rex factus est Lydiae.

[1]**pala,** *socket* (in which the stone of a ring is set)

34 When Bantius, a citizen of Nola, is planning to bring his fellow-citizens over to Hannibal's side, Marcellus prevents him by words of praise and by a gift

Claudius Marcellus, qui copiis Romanis in Campania praeerat, comperit[1] consilium L. Bantii Nolani, qui suos cives studebat corrumpere, ut, rebellione contra Romanos facta, ad Hannibalem deficerent. hoc facere cupivit Bantius quod, cum pugnans pro Romanis apud Cannas vulneratus esset, Hannibalis beneficio curatus erat et ex captivitate ad suos remissus erat. Marcellus Bantium interficere non audebat, ne morte eius reliquos Nolanos excitaret. Bantium igitur ad se arcessitum[2] allocutus est, dicens eum fortissimum militem esse, id quod affirmavit antea se ignoravisse. tum illum hortatus ut secum moraretur, et verbis laudavit et equum magnificum ei dedit. quo beneficio non illius solum fidem sed etiam omnium Nolanorum sibi confirmavit.

[1] **comperire,** *discover*   [2] **arcessere,** *summon*

35 Alcibiades the Athenian and Epaminondas the Theban illustrate different ways of taking a city

Alcibiades, dux Atheniensium, cum urbem egregie munitam obsideret, ab hostibus petiit facultatem consulendi de pacis condicionibus. qua facultate data, ipse urbem intravit, et in theatro, ubi locus consultationi, ut mos erat, dabatur et multi cives ad eum audiendum convenerant, diutissime loquebatur. atque, dum oratione sua multitudinem tenet, Athenienses, quos ad id praeparaverat, incustoditam urbem ceperunt. Epaminondas in Arcadia cognovit multas feminas die festo ambulare extra moenia urbis cuiusdam quam capere volebat. itaque inter hanc feminarum turbam immiscuit complures e militibus suis femineo vestitu. illi, sub noctem una cum feminis intra portas recepti, urbem ceperunt et suis aperuerunt.

36 Thirsty soldiers die from drinking too much water

Alexandri regis exercitus longum faciebat iter per loca deserta. cum deesset aqua, milites siti gravi oppressi sunt. tandem Alexander ipse ad flumen Oxum paullo ante solis occasum pervenit. sed exercitus magna pars nondum appropinquabat. itaque rex curavit ignes in alto monte accendendos, ut ei qui sequebantur cognoscerent castra haud procul abesse. simul imperat eis qui in primo agmine erant ut vasa implerent, quibus aqua ad reliquos milites portari posset sitis relevandae causa. sed multi biberunt tantum aquae ut, intercluso spiritu, mortui sint; ac numerus horum multo maior fuit quam rex ullo amiserat proelio.

How to tackle a Comprehension Passage

Comprehension Passage. Read it through once carefully.

For O-Level Latin, all the G.C.E. Boards prescribe, and have always prescribed, at least one Unseen as a compulsory exercise. The setting of Comprehension Passages is a comparative innovation. At present, only four Boards prescribe them as a compulsory exercise; two Boards don't set them at all; and the rest of the Boards make the working of them optional, the usual alternative being translation from English to Latin. It is as well to say at once that, given a choice between these alternatives, Comprehension Passages are not, in themselves, a soft option. Here are two facts which bear this out. First, it is by no means unusual for a candidate to get full marks in the O-Level examination for translation from English to Latin, whereas full marks for working a Comprehension Passage is something which very few candidates get near to achieving, and which hardly any achieve. Second, when candidates work two Unseens and a Comprehension Passage (a popular combination), they nearly always obtain their lowest mark on the Comprehension Passage. It would, of course, be quite wrong to offer any general advice about choice on the basis of these two facts. Each candidate is an individual. You may personally feel that your own knowledge of Latin is not sufficiently accurate for you to attempt translation from English to Latin; or, owing to shortage of time or for whatever other reason, you may have been given very little practice in translating from English to Latin. In either case, you choose, rightly, the Comprehension Passage. The advice which follows is both for those who, having an option, choose – whether rightly or wrongly – the Comprehension Passage, and of course for those who, having been entered for one of the G.C.E. Boards which make Comprehension Passages a compulsory exercise, have no choice to make.

The first, and highly important, point which must be made is that the advice which you have been given in *How to Tackle an Unseen* is equally valid here. You don't have to write out a translation of a

Comprehension Passage, but, if you can't translate it in your mind, you can't answer the questions set on it. Since the majority of these questions will have been set simply to test your understanding of the Latin, this Latin needs looking at just as closely as if you were asked to write down a translation. Marks are very frequently lost by failure to notice essential details. E.g., your answer may reveal that you failed to spot a tense correctly, took a superlative adjective to be a positive one, confused an indirect command with a purpose-clause, and so on. In short, any mistake which can be made in a written translation can reveal itself just as clearly in answers to questions set on a Comprehension Passage. The importance of close attention to the Latin cannot be over-emphasized, because the work of candidates in the O-Level examination provides clear proof that, when they come to tackle a Comprehension Passage, their concentration wavers. I recently marked the work of an O-Level candidate who had chosen to do two Unseens and the Comprehension Passage. He got 35/40 for one Unseen, 33/40 for the other. Having thus proved that his understanding of Latin was well above average, he went on to get 12/40 for the Comprehension Passage. This result is, admittedly, an extreme instance, but it does exemplify a general tendency, indisputably existing and already remarked upon, for candidates to get lower marks for the Comprehension Passage than for Unseens.

Lack of concentration on the Latin is not the only explanation of this tendency. Candidates also show an inability to cope with certain types of question commonly set – notably questions which are designed to test their knowledge of syntax and grammar. Characteristic questions of this type are those which ask for an explanation of a subjunctive or a case-usage, and those which ask the candidate to identify a part of a verb or to give the other degrees of comparison of an adjective or adverb. A surprisingly high proportion of candidates fail to cope with this type of question – and the marks dribble away. As regards these questions, neither grammar nor use of cases comes within the scope of this book; but you have earlier been given some incidental help, e.g., with the identification of infinitives and participles, and with one or two case-usages, such as the ablative absolute. Don't ignore this incidental help, but remember that questions involving grammar and case-usages are a test of your general knowledge of Latin and are not covered here. On the other hand, this book has given you much more than incidental help with one type of syntax-question which occurs frequently and which usually gets the worst answers of all – the question which asks why a particular verb is in the subjunctive. In answering this type of question, all that you are required to do is to produce the correct 'label', e.g., 'in a purpose clause', 'after a verb of fearing'. Since, in this book, you have already covered all the main subjunctive-constructions, you should have no difficulty with this type of question.

There are other types of question which can all too readily cause a loss of marks. Some of these will be looked at in the notes which are appended to the first three Comprehension Passages in this book; but two merit separate mention here: questions which test whether the candidate can spot a cross-reference, and questions which have to be answered by a Latin proper-noun in the nominative (this same proper-noun almost invariably occurring in the Comprehension Passage itself in some case other than the nominative). A single example will cover both these types of question. In one of the Comprehension Passages in this book, you will find the following question: '**Ducem** (line 14) – Give his name.' To answer this, candidates had to look back to the *first* line of the piece, where the name of the leader was to be found, in the ablative form **Cloelio**. When this Comprehension Passage was set at O Level, a considerable number of candidates couldn't cope with the cross-reference and offered no answer at all. They couldn't see the leader's name in the immediate vicinity and they didn't bother to look further away. Take a lesson from this, and remember that a question may, quite legitimately, be testing your understanding of the Comprehension Passage as a whole and may be requiring you to look backwards or forwards in order to find the answer. In the example we are looking at, a lot of candidates did realise this, but, having coped with the cross-reference, they spoiled their answer by writing it down as **Cloelio**. As the name of the leader was **Cloelius**, these candidates couldn't receive the 1 mark which the question carried. Their mistake seems childish. None the less, it represents a type of mistake which is made regularly, and by a great number of candidates.

One further point: for tackling Comprehension Passages you need a rather wider vocabulary than for Unseens. This applies particularly in the case of those G.C.E. Boards which set Comprehension Passages as an alternative to translation from English to Latin. If you have been given little or no practice in translating from English to Latin, you should have been able to compensate for this by wider reading in Latin, and, in this way, acquiring an adequate vocabulary. The greatest mistake you can make – and it is one that many O-Level candidates appear to make – is to think that, having avoided the rigorous concentration on details which translation from English to Latin demands, you can cast such concentration aside when you tackle a Comprehension Passage. In fact, just as much concentration on details is needed if you are to obtain marks comparable with those obtained by a careful and knowledgeable translator from English to Latin.

Notes have been appended to the first three Comprehension Passages. These three Passages, together with the next two, have not been set at O Level. Nos. 6–15 are the real thing: the pieces of Latin and the questions asked on them are printed here exactly as they appeared when they were set in the O-Level examination.

Comprehension Passages

Read the following passage carefully and then answer the
questions asked upon it. You are not required to write out a
translation unless specific questions ask for this.
(To save space, this rubric will not be printed at the head of
subsequent Comprehension Passages.)

1 **A pleasant surprise for a retired Roman general**
    P. Scipio, dux Romanus, qui multos hostes bello
devicerat, cum ad senectutem pervenisset in villam suam se
recepit. fama eius tanta erat ut plurimi eius visendi causa ad
villam iter facerent; inter quos quondam nonnulli praedonum[1]
duces, qui antea contra Romanos pugnaverant, eo   5
convenerunt. hos Scipio ad vim sibi faciendam venisse
existimavit; itaque praesidium collocavit servorum qui domum
defenderent, omniumque animi in praedonibus repellendis
occupabantur. quod ubi illi animadverterunt,
abiectis armis portae appropinquaverunt et clara voce   10
Scipioni nuntiaverunt se non eius hostes, sed virtutis
admiratores esse. haec postquam servi Scipioni rettulerunt,
portam aperiri eosque introduci iussit. praedones cupide eius
dextram apprehenderunt ac, positis ante vestibulum donis, laeti
quod virum tam praeclarum viderant, domum reverterunt.   15

[1] **praedo**, *a pirate*

Answer all the following questions:

a   **In villam suam se recepit** (lines 2/3). What stage of his life   1
    had Scipio reached when he did this?
b   **Fama eius tanta** (line 3). How had Scipio achieved this fame?   7
    What was the result of his fame after he retired to his villa?
c   **Praedonum duces** (lines 4/5). What information given about   3

these pirate-chiefs indicates that they were likely to be anti-Roman?

d	What did Scipio think was the purpose of the pirate-chiefs in coming to his villa?	3
e	What information, given later in this passage, about the equipment of the pirate-chiefs supports Scipio's view of their intention?	1
f	What precaution did Scipio take against them?	5
g	Translate **in praedonibus repellendis** (line 8).	2
h	What were the first two actions of the pirate-chiefs when they noticed the precaution taken against them?	4
i	Translate **nuntiaverunt . . . esse** (lines 11/12).	4
j	After hearing what the pirate-chiefs announced, what orders did Scipio give?	3
k	**Laeti . . . viderant** (lines 14/15). In what two ways had the pirate-chiefs just shown their admiration of Scipio?	5
l	What did the pirate-chiefs finally do?	2

Notes

a To get the one mark which this question carries, you need to know the meaning of one particular word in the Latin. The only precise English derivative of this is a very uncommon word, but there are kindred words which will help you.

b The first part of this question is designed to make you look back over a line or two. In answering the second part, don't miss the adjective in the superlative, and don't bungle the gerundive attraction, either here or in **d**.

e The information concerns equipment which the pirate-chiefs are later described as discarding – and which, therefore, they must previously have been carrying.

f To answer this question correctly, you will have to remember a particular use of the relative pronoun + subjunctive which was illustrated in the section on purpose clauses.

g There are no problems of vocabulary here. If you understand gerundive attraction, you should have no difficulty in getting full marks for this question.

h One of the actions is described by means of an ablative absolute. Describe it in English by using a main verb in the active.

i You are being asked to translate a perfectly straightforward example of acc. and inf.

j Having covered indirect commands, you should have no difficulty here.

k A knowledge of the ablative absolute is again required.

Since, like all the other Comprehension Passages in this book, this piece of Latin is an extract from a Latin author, it is a matter of chance that it contains three examples of gerundive attraction. It also contains, as my notes on the questions show, a mixture of other constructions. This one example of a Comprehension Passage should be sufficient, in itself, to convince you that a knowledge of Latin constructions is just as important here as it is with Unseens.

2 One man's courage leads to victory in a difficult situation

Caesar, ut Britannos vinceret, exercitum ad insulam transportaverat. sed militibus, e navibus in litus egredientibus, complures difficultates obstabant. nam oportebat eos ignotis locis, impeditis manibus, gravi onere armorum oppressos, in aquam desilire. cum igitur propter altitudinem maris   5 cunctarentur, miles quidam qui decimae legionis aquilam ferebat magna voce ceteros hortatus est ut se sequerentur, nisi vellent aquilam hostibus prodere. affirmavit se certe suum officium imperatori esse praestaturum[1]. quo dicto, se e navi proiecit atque in hostes aquilam ferre coepit. tum milites, ne   10 tantum dedecus[2] paterentur, universi e navi desiluerunt. pugnatum est acriter. Britanni, notis omnibus vadis[3], ubi aliquos milites e navi egredientes conspexerant, incitatis equis adoriebantur ac tela in eos undique coiciebant. Romani, simul atque in arido constiterunt, in hostes impetum fecerunt et   15 eos in fugam dederunt.

[1] **praestare officium**, *do one's duty*   [2] **dedecus**, *disgrace*
[3] **vadum**, *shoal*

Answer all the following questions:

a   **Ad insulam** (line 1). What had Caesar brought here and for   3
what purpose had he brought it?

b   **Complures difficultates** (line 3). What three particular   6
difficulties confronted the soldiers who would have to jump
down into the water?

c   **Cunctarentur** (line 6). What made the soldiers hesitate?   2

d   **Miles quidam** (line 6). In which legion was this soldier   1
serving as standard-bearer?

e   Write down, in its nominative singular, the Latin word which   2
is used in this extract to signify the standard. What does this
Latin word literally mean?

f   **Ceteros hortatus est** (line 7). What did the standard-bearer   5
exhort the rest to do? What did he imply would happen if they
refused to do as he said? How did he make sure that his
fellow-soldiers could hear him?

g   **Se certe . . . praestaturum** (lines 8/9). Give, in English, the   3
actual words which the standard-bearer used.

h   **Imperatori** (line 9). Give his name.   1

i   **Quo dicto** (line 9). Why are these two words in the ablative?   6
Having had his say, what two things did the standard-bearer
then do?

j   Translate **tum . . . desiluerunt** (lines 10/11).   5

k   **Britanni . . . adoriebantur** (lines 12/14). How did their   3
knowledge of the area help the Britons? What particular
advantage had they got over the disembarking Roman
foot-soldiers?

l   **In hostes impetum fecerunt** (line 15). The Romans made   2
this attack as soon as they were in a position to do so. What had
they to do in order to get themselves into this position?

m   What was the result of this attack?   1

Notes

b   A regular way of giving candidates the meaning of an unusual word is to incorporate its meaning in the wording of the question. Notice that the wording of this question gives you the meaning of **desilire**. You will need to remember this meaning when you tackle **j**.

c   As in **b**, the meaning of an unusual word, **cunctarentur**, has been incorporated in the wording of the question. In answering this question, don't be misled by an obvious English derivative. You will have no trouble if you know the two possible meanings of **altus**.

g   This type of question needs care. In this particular example, you are being asked to take the acc. and inf., a construction which, as you know, always *reports* what someone says or thinks, and, in your answer, to cut out the report-stage by getting back to the original words. Here is an example of the process required. **Puella se suos libros amisisse dixit** = *'the girl said that she had lost her books'*. It should be obvious that her original words were: **Amisi meos libros** = *'I have lost my books'*. In arriving at your answer, you have only to follow the process shown in this example, taking particular care to identify the tense of the infinitive correctly. In questions of this type, you must be prepared to meet indirect questions as an alternative to acc. and inf. Here is a sentence containing an indirect question: **Rogavit puerum quot naves vidisset**. A possible question would be: 'Give, in English, the actual words of the questioner.' The meaning of the Latin is: 'He asked the boy how many ships he had seen.' What the questioner actually said to the boy was: 'How many ships did you see/have you seen?' In **g**, you are asked to give your answer in English. Be prepared for a similar type of question in which you are asked to write down the answer in Latin.

k   Before answering the second half of this question, ask yourself why the setter has referred, here and here only, to the Roman legionaries as 'foot-soldiers'.

3 After the Roman defeat by the Carthaginians at Cannae, the Senate insists that a promise made to Hannibal must be kept

Post pugnam Cannensem, in qua Romani a Poenis victi sunt, trecenti Romani hostibus se dediderunt. his captivis Hannibal, Poenorum dux, libertatem promisit, si senatui Romano persuadere potuissent ut se maxima pecunia redimeret[1]. itaque e captivis decem delecti sunt qui Romam irent; qui omnes iuraverunt se ad Hannibalis castra redituros esse. sed cum castris egressi essent, unus eorum, quasi aliquid oblitus esset, in castra rediit, deinde ante noctem ceteros adsecutus est: ita enim putavit se iure iurando[2] liberavisse. cum decem captivi Romam venissent et rem nuntiavissent, senatores noluerunt eos redimere qui se dedidissent; itaque decretum est ut ad Hannibalem redirent. tum is qui iam antea in castra Poenorum redierat domum suam abiit. quod ubi Romani cognoverunt, omnes statuerunt eum comprehendendum et a custodibus ad Hannibalem deducendum esse.

[1] **redimere**, *ransom*   [2] **ius iurandum**, *oath*

Answer all the following questions:

Write down, in its nominative plural masculine, the Latin word which is used for 'Carthaginians' in this passage.   1

How many Romans surrendered to the enemy after the battle of Cannae?   1

What did Hannibal promise these prisoners? What did the prisoners have to do before his promise could be fulfilled?   8

How many prisoners were then picked out and for what purpose?   3

What did these picked men all swear to do?   3

Translate **cum castris egressi essent** (line 7).   2

Unus eorum (line 7). On what pretext did this man return to Hannibal's camp? **Ante noctem** (line 8). What did he succeed in doing before night-fall? What did he think he had achieved by his return to the camp?   6

Cum . . . venissent (line 10). After reaching Rome, what did these prisoners do?   2

Senatores noluerunt (line 11). What did the senators refuse to do? What course of action was then decreed for the prisoners who had come to Rome?   4

Which one of the prisoners ignored this decree? What did he do instead?   5

When his action was discovered, what did the Romans universally decide must be done with him?   4

Quod ubi Romani cognoverunt (lines 13/14). Write down, in the appropriate gender, number, and case, a Latin word which could have been used instead of **quod** in this phrase.   1

Notes

The English title provides the clue here.
This is a type of question which is quite often set. In *How to Tackle an Unseen* (pp. 11/12) you were shown, in effect, how to answer such questions.

4 Apollo's ambiguous oracle leads Pyrrhus to defeat

Pyrrhus, rex Epiri, cum imperium omnium gentium
cuperet et Romanos se in hac re impedire videret, oraculum
Apollinis de bello contra eos gerendo consuluit; cui a deo
ambigue responsum est:

Armis te dico Romanos vincere posse.

Pyrrhus, homo superbus, putavit deum sibi victoriam
promittere. itaque bellum Romanis intulit et consulem
Laevinum exercitumque eius superavit. sed in hac pugna
permultos suorum amisit; itaque amicis gratulantibus 'Quid'
inquit 'mihi prodest[1] talis victoria?' cum autem omnes
Romanos adversis[2] vulneribus occisos videret, 'Ego' inquit 'si
tales viros haberem, totum orbem terrarum superare
potuissem.' deinde, cum eundem Laevinum cum altero
exercitu sibi oppositum invenisset, 'Eadem' inquit 'est fortuna
mihi adversus Romanos quae olim fuit Herculi adversus
Hydram'. Hydra enim tale erat monstrum ut, cum caput esset
abscissum, plura capita statim ex eius collo apparerent.
Pyrrhus postea a Romanis victus, quid Apollo oraculo suo
dicere voluisset, tandem cognovit.

[1] **prodesse**, *be of use*   [2] **adversus**, *adj ., on the front of the body*

Answer all the following questions:

What ambition did Pyrrhus have and whom did he see as hindering its fulfilment? **3**

Consuluit (line 3). Whose oracle did he consult? On what did he want advice? **3**

A deo ambigue responsum est (lines 3/4). Translate the god's ambiguous reply in the two possible ways. **3**

What did Pyrrhus think that the god was promising him? Why did he think this? **2**

What action did Pyrrhus then take? What was his first achievement after taking this action? **5**

'Quid mihi prodest talis victoria?' (lines 9/10). Translate these words. What reason did Pyrrhus have for disparaging his victory? **6**

Cum . . . videret (lines 10/11). What proof of Roman bravery did Pyrrhus see here? **3**

Si tales viros haberem (lines 11/12). What did Pyrrhus think he could have done if he had men like these? **2**

Sibi oppositum (line 14). Name the person to whom **sibi** refers. Write down the present infinitive active of the verb of which **oppositum** is a part. **2**

'Eadem . . . Hydram' (lines 14/16). To what hero of mythology is Pyrrhus comparing himself? What opponent had confronted this hero? Who are confronting Pyrrhus? **3**

Cum caput esset abscissum (lines 16/17). After the Hydra's head had been cut off, what immediately appeared out of its neck? **2**

In what way was Pyrrhus comparing Laevinus and the Romans with the Hydra? **4**

Tandem cognovit (line 19). What, as Pyrrhus finally discovered, had the god wanted to tell him by means of his oracle? **2**

5 Latinus receives Aeneas in Laurentine territory

Troia capta Aeneas, domo profugus, primo in
Macedoniam venit; inde in Siciliam, quaerens locum ubi urbem
condere posset, delatus est; ab Sicilia ad Laurentem agrum
navigavit. cum ibi egressi Troiani, quibus nihil praeter arma et
naves supererat, praedam ex agris agerent, Latinus rex
Aboriginesque, qui tum ea tenebant loca, ad arcendam[1] vim
advenarum[2] armati ex urbe atque agris concurrunt. cum
instructae acies constitissent, priusquam signum proelii
committendi daretur, processit Latinus ducemque advenarum
evocavit ad colloquium. percontatus[3] qui essent
quidve quaerentes in agrum Laurentem venissent,
postquam audivit homines esse Troianos et ducem Aeneam,
filium Anchisae et Veneris, rex, admiratus viri nobilitatem et
animum vel bello vel paci paratum, dextra data eum in
amicitiam recepit. inde foedus factum inter duces, inter
exercitus salutatio facta est.

[1] **arcere**, *ward off*   [2] **advena**, *a stranger*   [3] **percontor**, *ask*

Answer all the following questions:

Troia capta (line 1). In what case are these two words? Why   2
are they in that case?

Before reaching the Laurentine territory, what island did   1
Aeneas come to?

Quaerens locum (line 2). Who was doing this and for what   3
purpose?

Troiani (line 4). What had these men got left in the way of   4
possessions? How did they attempt to replenish their supplies?

Aborigines (line 6). What does this word mean when used as   3
an English word? Write down the two Latin words of which it
is composed.

Armati . . . concurrunt (line 7). For what purpose were these   3
men rallying together?

Instructae acies (line 8). Whose lines of battle are referred   3
to ? Write down in its present infinitive passive the verb of
which **instructae** is a part.

Translate the phrase **signum proelii committendi** (lines   2
8/9).

Ducemque advenarum evocavit (lines 9/10). Who is this   2
leader? For what purpose did Latinus invite him to step
forward?

Percontatus (line 10). What information did the questioner,   4
Latinus, seek to obtain?

Why is **venissent** (line 11) in the subjunctive?   1

What did Latinus find out about the nationality of the   3
'strangers' and about the parentage of their leader?

Viri (line 13). Who is this man? What qualities did Latinus find   5
to admire in him?

Eum in amicitiam recepit (lines 14/15). What outward sign of   2
this friendly reception did Latinus give?

What then took place (i) between the two leaders (ii) between   2
the two armies?

6 A king forces a mother to acknowledge her son

Civis quidam mortuus est. reliquit uxorem et filium qui, vix unum annum natus, matrem non noverat. quia mater pauper erat, filius ab aliquo in aliam provinciam ductus est, ut ibi educaretur. factus iuvenis ad matrem rediit. quem cum mater vidisset, gratias dis egit quod filius regressus erat. sed mater nuper sponsa[1] erat novo viro; qui viso iuvene rogavit quis esset. ubi intellexit eum sponsae mulieris filium esse, iratus 'aut tu nega filium tuum esse,' inquit, 'aut ego abibo hinc.' tum mater territa dixit filio: 'vade, iuvenis, ex mea domo in quam te ignotum accepi.' quid multa? iuvenis adiit regem, cui omnia narravit. rex matrem arcessitam rogavit: 'mulier, quid dicis? est tuus filius an non?' illa respondit: 'non est meus filius sed eum accepi quia pauper est.' tum rex mulierem rogavit quantam pecuniam ipsa haberet. respondit: 'usque ad mille solidos.' tum rex, 'dicis iuvenem pauperem esse,' inquit, 'sed tu ipsa ditissima es, neque tibi est coniunx. tibi impero igitur ut huic iuveni sine mora nubas.' tum mulier confusa iuvenem filium suum esse confessa est.

[1] **sponderi**, *to become engaged to*

Answer all the following questions:

a   Give the meaning of **vix** (line 2).   1
b   Why, at this point in the story, did the son not know his mother?   2
c   Why is the phrase **unum annum** (line 2) in the accusative case?   1
d   Why were mother and son separated? Where was the son taken to and for what purpose?   2, 2
e   How should **quem** (line 4) be translated?   1
f   How did the mother react to her son's return?   3
g   Translate **sed mater . . . quis esset** (lines 5–7).   4
h   Why is **esset** (line 7) in the subjunctive?   1
i   Why did the mother's fiancé get angry?   2
j   What alternatives did he then offer to the mother?   2
k   Substitute for **vade** (line 9) the corresponding part of **eo**.   1
l   Why did the mother use the word **iuvenis** (line 9)?   1
m   'To cut a long story short': give the Latin phrase (occurring in the passage) which is the equivalent of this English phrase. Translate the Latin phrase literally.   3
n   Translate **rex matrem arcessitam rogavit** (line 11).   3
o   After denying to the king that the young man was her son, what reason did the mother give for having received him into her house as a stranger?   1
p   **Quantam pecuniam ipsa haberet** (line 14). What, in Latin, were the actual words of the king?   2
q   **Solidos** (line 15) means 'gold coins'; but how did the word feature in the pre-decimal monetary system of Great Britain?   2
r   **Ditissima** (line 16). Give the other degrees of comparison of this adjective.   2
s   How did the king finally force the mother to acknowledge her son?   4

7

The Boeotians, having become unwilling allies of the Romans in their war against King Philip of Macedon, elect as Boeotarch Brachyllas, an anti-Roman, whose murder is subsequently contrived by two of his disappointed rivals

Dum Romani bellum contra regem Philippum gerebant, Boeotorum maior pars regi favebant, e quibus multi cum exercitu eius militabant. interea tamen ceteri Boeoti a Flaminino, duce Romano, vi coacti in societatem Romanam inierant. Philippo tandem superato, hibernabat Elatiae Flamininus, a quo Boeoti petierunt ut ei qui suae gentis in exercitu regis militavissent sibi redderentur. id a Flaminino facile impetratum est[1] quia favorem omnium Graecorum ad se convertere cupiebat. at, redditis eis, Boeoti videbantur nullam gratiam erga Flamininum habere, et Brachyllam quendam Boeotarchum fecerunt propter nullam aliam causam quam quod dux fuerat Boeotorum pro rege pugnantium, et reiecerunt Zeuxippum et Pisistratum, cives clarissimos, qui Romanae societatis auctores fuerant. hi non modo in praesentia sunt irati quod essent reiecti, sed etiam in futurum ceperunt metum ne profectis in Italiam Romanis ipsi interficerentur. itaque dum Romanum exercitum in propinquo haberent, Brachyllam necare constituerunt; nec multo post, cum ille e concilio publico domum reverteretur, circumventus occiditur ab sex armatis. comites eius fugerunt; interfectores proxima porta evaserunt.

[1] **impetrare**, *gain a request*

Answer all the following questions:

a What side did most of the Boeotians support? What practical proof did some of them give of this support?   2

b Why did the rest of the Boeotians make the alliance they did?   1

c What is the construction of **Philippo superato** (line 5)?   1

d In what case is the place-name **Elatiae** (line 5)? What was Flamininus doing at this place?   2

e What request did the Boeotians make to Flamininus?   4

f What does **a** (line 6) mean?   1

g Why did Flamininus yield to the Boeotians' request?   3

h Translate **Boeoti . . . habere** (lines 9/10).   3

i Write down, in the form in which it occurs here, the Latin word which shows that Brachyllas was a person of no particular importance. Give the meaning of this Latin word.   2

j Why did the Boeotians elect Brachyllas as Boeotarch (chief magistrate of the Boeotians)?   2

k What reason is implied for the rejection, in this election, of two eminent citizens?   2

l **Cives** (line 13). Give the names of these men in their nominative forms.   2

m **Clarissimos** (line 13). Give, in the nominative singular masculine, the other degrees of comparison of this word.   2

n What was the immediate reaction of these citizens to the election of Brachyllas? What fear did these citizens have for the future, and why did they have this fear?   4

o What did these citizens decide to do and what circumstance led them not to delay?   3

p How many men attacked Brachyllas? What was he doing when he was attacked?   4

q By what exit did the attackers leave the city?   2

8 Murder at an inn is disclosed by a dream

Cum duo fratres Athenienses, Philippus et Alexander,
iter una facerent et Megaram venissent, Philippus ad tabernam
iit, Alexander ad amici domum. cum hic media nocte
dormiret, in somnio ille alter ei apparuit oravitque ut
subveniret, quod sibi a caupone mors pararetur. quo somnio   5
Alexander excitatus est. sed cum se collegisset, putavit
somnium pro nihilo habendum esse, atque mox in somnum
relapsus est. tum ei dormienti, imago Philippi visa est rogare
ut, quoniam sibi vivo non subvenisset, mortem suam
ulcisceretur. 'interfectus' inquit 'a caupone et in agricolae   10
cuiusdam plaustrum iactus, extra portam efferor.' magnopere
commotus, Alexander ad urbis portam mane contendit.
plaustro viso, quo agricola vehebatur, quaesivit ex eo quid
plaustro inesset. ille aufugit; Philippus mortuus in plaustro
inventus est; caupo is coniectus est in carcerem.   15

Answer all the following questions:

a **Duo fratres** (line 1). To what city did they belong? What does **una** (line 2) mean? What place had the brothers now reached? 3

b Where did Philippus go when the brothers parted company for the night? 1

c **Hic** (line 3). In whose house was he? What was he doing and at what time? 3

d **Ille alter** (line 4). Who was he? In what way did he appear and to whom? 3

e **Oravit** (line 4). What request did he make and what reason did he give for making it? 3

f **Quo** (line 5). Give a Latin word, in the appropriate case, number and gender, which could have been used instead of this word. 1

g **Somnio** (line 5). What was the immediate effect of this on Alexander? 1

h Translate **cum se collegisset** (line 6). 2

i What did Alexander think about the **somnium**, and with what result? 4

j **Imago Philippi** (line 8). How would you translate **imago** here? What request and what reproach did the **imago** make? 5

k **Mortem suam** (line 9). Why does the writer use **suam** here, and not **eius**? 1

l Translate **Interfectus . . . efferor** (lines 10/11). 6

m **Contendit** (line 12). To what place and at what time? 2

n **Quaesivit ex eo** (line 13). Give, in English, the actual question as it was asked at the time. 2

o What was the farmer's reaction to this question? 1

p What then happened to the inn-keeper? 2

9 The chariots of Archelaus prove ineffective against Sulla's counter-measures

Archelaus adversus L. Sullam in fronte ad perturbandum hostem quadrigas[1] locavit, in secunda acie Macedones, in tertia armatos auxiliares, mixtis fugitivis Italicae gentis, quorum virtuti plurimum fidebat. in utroque deinde latere equites, quorum amplum numerum habebat, circumeundi   5
hostis causa posuit. contra haec Sulla fossas amplae latitudinis utroque latere duxit quas castellis munivit. ita effecit ne circumiretur ab hoste et peditum numero et equitum superante. triplicem deinde peditum aciem instruxit, relictis intervallis per quae levem armaturam et equites emitteret.   10
tum militibus qui in secunda acie erant imperavit ut quam plurimos palos[2] firme in terram defigerent. atque, cum quadrigae appropinquarent, recepit intra palos[2] milites primae aciei. tum demum sublato universorum clamore levem armaturam iacere tela iussit. quibus factis, quadrigae   15
hostium, aut implicitae[3] palis[2] aut exterritae clamore telisque, in suos conversae sunt turbaveruntque Macedonum ordines, quibus cedentibus, cum Sulla instaret, contra eum Archelaus equites instruxit. quos Romani equites subito emissi averterunt consummaveruntque victoriam.   20

[1] **quadriga** *can denote either a chariot or a team of four horses which draws the chariot*   [2] **palus**, *a (pointed) stake*   [3] **implicitus**, *entangled*

a	Where did Archelaus position his chariots and for what purpose?	2
b	Who composed his second line?	1
c	Give in the appropriate case the Latin word to be understood with **tertia** (line 3).	1
d	Of what race were the runaways whom Archelaus mixed with his auxiliary troops? What was his attitude towards them?	3
e	Give the other degrees of comparison of **plurimum** (line 4).	2
f	Where did Archelaus position his cavalry and for what purpose?	3
g	What measures, in the way of groundworks and fortifications, did Sulla adopt when confronted by the army of Archelaus?	5
h	What did he achieve by these measures? What advantages had the enemy got which made these measures necessary?	4
i	With what Latin word in the passage does **superante** (line 9) agree?	1
j	How many ranks were there in Sulla's battle-line of infantry? Why did he leave gaps in this line?	3
k	What order did Sulla give to his troops who were in the second line?	3
l	What action did Sulla take when the enemy's chariots were approaching?	2
m	What did Sulla order his light-armed troops to do after a general battle-cry was raised?	1
n	What happened to the chariots of Archelaus and what effect did they have on the Macedonian ranks?	5
o	When Sulla was advancing, with what troops did Archelaus confront him?	1
p	What counter-measure was taken by the Romans and with what result?	3

10 Alcibiades offers good advice, which is not accepted

Pulsus in exsilium ab Atheniensibus Alcibiades se contulit
in Chersonesum, atque, dum ibi habitat, magnam amicitiam
sibi cum Seuthe rege Thraciae peperit. neque tamen se
Atheniensem esse oblivisci potuit, atque quamquam exsul erat
vehementer studebat iuvare Athenienses in bello quod   5
contra Lacedaemonios gerebant. nam eo tempore Philocles
imperator Atheniensium classem suam apud Aegos flumen
constituerat nec longe aberat Lysander imperator
Lacedaemoniorum. itaque Alcibiades ad Philoclem venit
atque ei monstravit Lysandrum in eo esse occupatum ut   10
bellum quam diutissime protraheret. pecuniam enim
suppeditari[1] Lacedaemoniis a rege Persarum, Atheniensibus
tamen nihil praeter naves superesse. affirmavit igitur
Lysandrum nolle statim pugnare quod pedestribus copiis plus
quam navibus valeret, et promisit se coacturum   15
Lysandrum aut mari dimicare aut pacem petere; se hoc facile
confecturum persuadendo Seuthi ut illum e terra expelleret.
Philocles autem noluit consilium Alcibiadis accipere quod
putavit Alcibiadi laudem futuram esse si quid secundi[2]
evenisset, sibi ipsi culpam si quid adversi accidisset. ab   20
hoc discedens Alcibiades 'te moneo' inquit 'ne iuxta hostes
castra habeas nautica; timeo enim ne immodestia vestrorum
militum occasio detur Lysandro superandi vestri exercitus.'
atque ea res sic evenit ut putaverat Alcibiades; nam Lysander,
cum per speculatores intellexisset Athenienses   25
in terram praedatum exisse navesque paene inanes relictas,
sine mora totam classem Atheniensem cepit eoque impetu
bellum totum finiit.

[1] **suppeditare**, *supply*   [2] **secundum**, *success*

Answer all the following questions:

a Why did Alcibiades leave Athens and where did he then go? 2
b Name the man whom he made his friend. 1
c What part of what verb is **peperit** (line 3)? 2
d With whom were the Athenians fighting a war at the time? 1
e What fact was Alcibiades, in exile, unable to forget? What attitude did this fact make him adopt in the war? 3
f Who were Philocles and Lysander? 2
g Translate **atque ei . . . protraheret** (lines 10/11). 4
h From whom were the Lacedaemonians getting money? 1
i What resources did the Athenians still possess? 2
j Why, according to Alcibiades, was Lysander unwilling to fight at once? 2
k What promise did Alcibiades make to Philocles and how did he propose to fulfil that promise? 4
l Who was Seuthes? 1
m What did Philocles think would result from acceptance of Alcibiades' plan (i) if it succeeded (ii) if it failed? 2
n What warning did Alcibiades give to Philocles? What did he fear might be the consequence of the lack of discipline among Philocles' troops? 4
o Why are (i) **habeas** (line 22) and (ii) **detur** (line 23) in the subjunctive? 2
p What did Lysander discover by means of his scouts? 4
q What part of the verb is **praedatum** (line 26)? 1
r Why was this the decisive battle in the war? 2

11 Romulus, of ancient descent, survives Amulius' attempt on his life; is successful over his brother Remus in bird-observation; becomes king of Rome; and, after beginning the building of its first defensive wall, kills his brother, Remus

Troia flammis deleta, Aeneas cum multis Troianis in
Italiam venit atque, cum Aborigines bello superavisset,
regnavit in Latio. multis post annis natus est Romulus, Romae
conditor, cuius mater erat Rhea, prognata ex Aeneae gente.
patrem eius Rhea confessa est Martem esse; atque postea
omnes hoc libenter crediderunt. nam, cum Romulus una cum
Remo fratre in flumen Tiberim iactus esset iussis Amulii, qui
tum in Latio regnabat, feliciter servatus est. non modo Tiberis
infantes ad ripam incolumes portavit sed etiam lupa, secuta
eorum clamores, ubera dedit[1]. repertos in silva Faustulus
pastor tulit in suam casam atque educavit. Alba tum Latio
caput erat, urbs aedificata ab Iulo quod contempserat
Lavinium urbem patris Aeneae. Amulius expulerat fratrem
Numitorem, Rheae patrem, atque tali modo regnum nactus
erat. Romulus igitur primo iuventutis ardore patruum
expulit, avum reposuit. deinde novam urbem cum fratre
Remo condere statuit, et, quod fratres gemini erant, placuit eis
petere a deis uter regeret. Remus montem Aventinum,
Romulus Palatinum occupabat atque uterque signum divinum
exspectabat. mox ille sex vulturios, hic duodecim vidit. sic
victor Romulus urbem aedificare coepit, sperans eam
bellatricem fore; id enim promittebant vulturii, aves praedam
capere solitae. ad muniendam novam urbem vallum sufficere
videbatur; sed cum Remus ridens trans vallum parvum
saltavisset, occisus est a fratre irato.

[1] **ubera dare**, *suckle*

Answer all the following questions:

How was Troy destroyed? 1

In what part of Italy did Aeneas rule? 1

Explain the meaning of the word **Aborigines** (line 2), giving 3
the two Latin words from which it is derived.

What part of speech is **post** (line 3)? 1

Who was the mother of Romulus and from whom was she 2
descended?

Translate **patrem . . . Martem esse** (line 5). 3

What did Amulius order to be done to Romulus and Remus? 2

Before their discovery by the shepherd Faustulus, the lives of 4
Romulus and Remus were saved by two happenings. Describe
each of these happenings.

What was the capital city of Latium at this time? Who had built 4
it and why?

Translate **Romulus . . . reposuit** (lines 15/16). 3

Give the names of the men referred to as **patruum** and **avum**. 2

Romulus and Remus decided to ask the gods a question. What 2
was the question and why had it arisen?

Why is **regeret** (line 18) in the subjunctive? 1

Which two of Rome's seven hills are mentioned at this point in 2
the story?

Romulus is described as **victor** (line 21). In what way was he 2
victorious over his brother?

What hope did Romulus have for the city which he began to 3
build? What reason was there for his thinking that this hope
would be fulfilled?

Translate **ad muniendam novam urbem** (line 23). 2

Why did Romulus kill his brother Remus? 2

12

The emperor Valentinianus, who, together with Sebastianus, is attacking the Alamanni, finds that this tribe has taken up a position on a mountain accessible only on one side. On a reconnoitring expedition, the emperor has a narrow escape

Cum imperator Valentinianus una cum legato Sebastiano contra Alamannos progrederetur, primo nullus hostis qui resisteret inveniri potuit. sed cum imperator ad locum venisset cui nomen Solicinio est, iussit exercitum consistere. doctus enim erat barbaros longe conspectos esse. mox cognovit per exploratores Alamannos occupavisse montem altissimum cui nullus accessus esset nisi septentrionali latere, unde declivitatem haberet facilem et mollem. itaque Valentinianus Sebastiano imperavit ut hanc partem montis cum suis occuparet, oppugnaturus Alamannos si forte fugientes ab hoc latere exissent. ipse cum decem militibus, quorum fidem noverat, et uno servo profectus est ut imas partes montis circumspiceret. ac putavit (erat enim sui arrogans aestimator) se ipsum invenire posse aliam viam ad summum montem ducentem, praeter eam quam perspexerant exploratores. ac dum per loca palustria iter facit, subito oppugnatus est a barbaris qui in insidiis latebant, neque effugisset nisi equo incitato quam celerrime ad suas legiones properavisset. sed servus, qui portabat imperatoris galeam[1] auro argentoque ornatam, interiit[2] cum ipsa galea[1] nec postea repertus est aut vivus aut mortuus.

[1] **galea**, *helmet*   [2] **interire**, *be lost, disappear*

Answer all the following questions:

What position did Sebastianus hold?	1
Why was the first stage of the emperor's advance an easy one?	2
When the emperor reached Solicinium, what order did he give to his army?	1
Why did he give this order?	3
Describe the geographical features of the mountain which the Alamanni had seized.	6
How had the emperor obtained his information about the mountain?	1
What order did the emperor give to Sebastianus and for what purpose was Sebastianus to hold himself in readiness?	6
How many soldiers did the emperor take with him on his reconnaissance and why had he picked these particular men?	2
What other person was a member of this party?	1
What area did the emperor set out to reconnoitre?	2
What did he think he could find in the course of this reconnaissance?	3
Pick out and write down in Latin a phrase which illustrates the emperor's self-confidence. Translate this phrase into English.	3
What sort of country did the emperor and his reconnaissance-party make their way through?	1
Subito oppugnatus est (lines 16/17). Why was the emperor taken by surprise?	2
Describe the emperor's escape.	3
Although the emperor escaped, in what way was this an expensive day for him?	3

13 The emperor Anastasius, after his first method of choosing a successor has failed, is shown, by divine intervention, a second method

Eo tempore Anastasius imperator habebat tres parvos nepotes, Pompeium, Probum et Hypatium. cogitans quem ex his faceret post se imperatorem, quodam die iussit eos secum prandere, et intra palatium post prandium meridiari[1]. tum singulos lectos[2] eis poni iussit, et in uno lecto ad caput celari regium insigne[3]. nam putabat eum ex nepotibus qui hunc lectum elegisset futurum esse illum cui regnum postea traderet. et post prandium unus quidem in unum lectum se iecit, sed duo in alio lecto propter amorem fraternum una se collocaverunt. itaque accidit ut in illo lecto ubi regium insigne positum erat nemo eorum dormiret. cum hoc modo cognovisset neminem nepotum regnaturum esse, Anastasius coepit orare deos ut signum sibi darent, quo scire posset, dum adhuc viveret, quis post mortem suam regnum accepturus esset. tum, post breve temporis intervallum, noctu vidit in somnio hominem qui ita ei locutus est: 'qui cras tibi primus in cubiculum introductus erit, is accipiet post te tuum regnum.' ita factum est ut Iustinus, qui praefectus urbis erat, ei primus introduceretur a servo qui imperatoris cubiculo praeerat. tum Anastasius egit gratias deis, qui successorem ostendissent.

[1] **meridiari**, *take a siesta*   [2] **lectus**, *bed*
[3] **regium insigne**, *symbol of royalty*

Answer all the following questions:

What relation was Anastasius to Pompeius, Probus, and Hypatius?   1

Cogitans . . . imperatorem (lines 2/3). Translate these words.   4

In what mood and tense is **elegisset** (line 7)? Account for the mood.   3

As a preliminary to solving this problem, Anastasius ordered four things to be done. What were they?   6

How did Anastasius think that his problem would now be solved?   4

What did the young boys then do, and why did their actions cause Anastasius' plan to fail?   5

After the failure of his first plan, Anastasius prayed. What was his prayer?   4

Why are **posset** (line 13) and **accepturus esset** (lines 14/15) in the subjunctive?   2

Vidit . . . hominem (lines 15/16). Was Anastasius asleep or awake when he saw this man?   1

Translate the statement which the man gave in lines 16/17 (**qui cras . . . regnum**).   4

What was the name of the man finally revealed as successor to Anastasius? What office did he hold? Who admitted him to Anastasius' presence?   4

What did Anastasius do when his problem was settled?   2

14 A Roman consul defeats the Volsci

Volsci duce Cloelio Ardeam venerunt et contra moenia
vallum aedificaverunt. quod ubi Romam est nuntiatum, M.
Geganius consul, cum exercitu profectus, tria milia passuum a
Volscis locum castris cepit. primis tenebris cibum capere
milites iussit. deinde quarta vigilia ipsos Volscos vallo
circumdare coepit; quod opus tam celeriter confectum est ut
sole orto Volsci se firmiore munitione ab Romanis
circumdatos quam a se urbem viderent. Volscorum dux ad
eam diem frumento ex agris rapto milites aluerat[1]. itaque,
postquam circummunitus omnium rerum inopiam pati
coepit, ad colloquium consulem evocavit ac dixit se Volscos
abducturum esse si Romani obsidionem omitterent[2]. ad haec
respondit consul accipiendas esse victis condiciones: tradi
ducem, arma deponi iussit. Volsci has condiciones accipere
noluerunt atque arma sumpserunt. sed aggressi
Romanos loco ad pugnam iniquo, iniquiore ad fugam, cum ab
omni parte caederentur, a proelio ad preces versi sunt. dedito
duce traditisque armis dimissi sunt. et cum prope urbem
Tusculum consedissent, propter veterem inimicitiam a
Tusculanis inermes oppugnati sunt. consul triumphans in
urbem redit.

[1] **alere**, *feed*   [2] **omittere**, *abandon*

Answer all the following questions:

What does the absence of a preposition with **Ardeam** (line 1)   1
tell you about this word?

Quod . . . nuntiatum (line 2). Translate this phrase. Why is   4
Romam in the accusative case?

How far away from the Volsci did the consul pitch his camp?   2

Cibum . . . iussit (lines 4/5). Re-write this phrase in Latin,   4
using, instead of **iussit**, the verb **impero** in its appropriate part
and with its appropriate construction.

Primis tenebris . . . coepit (lines 4–6). Quote in Latin and   4
translate into English two phrases in these sentences which
show that, at this point in the narrative, it was night, not day.

Volsci . . . viderent (lines 7/8). What did the Volsci realize at   3
this point?

Up to that day, how had the Volscian leader got food for his   3
men?

Ad colloquium consulem evocavit (line 11). What led the   3
leader of the Volsci to do this?

Se Volscos abducturum esse (lines 11/12). Give, in English,   2
the actual words used by the leader of the Volsci.

In what case is **victis** (line 13) and why?   2

Ducem (line 14). Give his name.   1

Loco (line 16). How does the author describe this place as   3
contributing to the defeat and surrender of the Volsci?

Translate **ad preces versi sunt** (line 17).   2

Dedito duce (lines 17/18). What construction is this?   1

Why ought the Volsci to have known better than to take up a   4
position near Tusculum? Why had they no chance of defending
themselves?

Consul . . . in urbem redit (lines 20/21). What city was this?   1

15 Hannibal transports elephants across the river Rhone

Milites Hannibalis flumen Rhodanum facile transierunt. traicere elephantos erat multo difficilius. quidam scriptores sic narrant: elephantus ferocissimus duxit in aquam ceteros, qui hunc ducem secuti ad alteram ripam ipso fluminis impetu rapti sunt. sed magis constat elephantos ratibus traiectos esse. porrexerunt in flumen ratem unam ducentos pedes longam, quinquaginta latam, ad ripam validis catenis vinctam. huic rati humum iniecerunt ut elephanti audacter velut per solum ingrederentur. altera ratis, longa pedes centum et ad flumen transeundum apta, primae iuncta est. tum elephanti, feminis ducentibus, acti sunt in primam ratem. cum haec stabilis esset, omnes sine timore progressi sunt in alteram, quae statim resoluta ad alteram ripam ab navibus quibusdam tracta est. primis expositis, alii deinde traiecti sunt. tres elephanti in flumen ceciderunt; sed, cum pondere ipso stabiles essent, in terram tuti pervenere.

Answer all the following questions:

a	Translate **traicere . . . difficilius** (line 2).	3
b	The author describes two ways in which the elephants may have been got across the Rhone. Describe the first of these ways; say whether you think it would have been possible, and, if you do not think so, say why not.	6
c	The second method was transportation by raft. How long and how wide was the first raft?	2
d	**Validis catenis vinctam** (line 7). Why do you think that this was necessary?	2
e	What does the author say was the purpose of throwing earth on the first raft?	3
f	What part of what verb is **ingrederentur** (line 9)?	2
g	Translate **ad flumen transeundum apta** (lines 9/10).	2
h	**Feminis ducentibus** (lines 10/11). What construction is this?	1
i	What part of what verb is **acti sunt** (line 11)?	2
j	Why did the elephants move without fear from the first raft to the second?	2
k	What two actions were then taken?	4
l	Suggest a reason why the preposition **ab** is used with **navibus** (line 13).	2
m	**Primis expositis** (line 14). Translate this phrase.	2
n	What mishap befell three of the elephants?	2
o	What physical characteristic was helpful in getting these three to safety?	2
p	**Pervenere** (line 16). Give the more usual form of this word.	1
q	Give an example, quoting it in Latin, of an accusative and infinitive construction taken from this passage.	2

Appendix A

Military Vocabulary

acies, *line of battle*
adsequi/consequi, *catch up with/overtake*
aggredi/adoriri, *attack*
agmen, *column (on the march)*
appropinquare, *approach*
arma tradere, *hand over arms*
armatus, *armed*
auxilia, *(neut. plur.), auxiliary troops*
auxilium, *a help*
bellum gerere, *wage/carry on/conduct war*
bellum indicere, *declare war*
castra ponere, *pitch camp*
cingere/circumdare, *surround*
clam, *secretly*
cognoscere, *to learn, find out*
commeatus/res frumentaria, *food-supply*
conficere, *complete, finish off*
consistere, *halt*
contendere/iter facere, *march*
copiae, *forces*
custodire, *guard*
custos, *a guard*
deditio, *a surrender*
deducere, *lead away/withdraw*
delere, *destroy*
discedere, *depart*
discessus, *departure*
ducere, *lead*
educere, *lead out*
effugere, *escape*
emittere, *send out*
eques, *a cavalryman*
equitatus, *cavalry*
erumpere, *break out*
eruptio, *a break out*
exercitus, *army*
expugnare, *take by storm*
foedus –eris, *a treaty*

fossa, *ditch/trench*
fugare, *put to flight*
fugere, *flee*
galea, *helmet*
gladius, *sword*
hasta, *spear*
haud procul, *not far off*
idoneus, *suitable*
impedimenta, *(neut. plur.), baggage*
impedimentum, *a hindrance*
imperator, *emperor (and see **legatus**)*
incolumis/tutus, *safe/unharmed*
insidiae, *an ambush*
instruere, *draw up*
intercludere, *cut off (supplies etc.)*
interficere/necare/caedere/occidere, *kill*
interrumpere, *break down (a bridge etc.)*
iter, *march, journey*
legatus, *two distinct meanings (a) an ambassador (b) a general, serving under a Commander-in-Chief who will be called **imperator***
magnum iter, *a forced march*
novae copiae, *reinforcements*
obsidere, *besiege*
obsidio, *a siege*
obviam ire, *go to meet/encounter*
occupare, *seize*
opprimere, *crush*
oppugnare, *attack/assault (esp. of towns)*
palam, *openly*
pauci, *a few*
pedes, *an infantryman*
peditatus, *infantry*
pellere, repellere, *drive back*
perficere, *complete*
pilum, *pike*
praeesse, *be in charge*

praefectus, *commander*
praeficere, *put in charge*
praemittere, *send forward*
praesidium, *garrison/guard*
procul, *at a distance*
proelium committere, *join battle*
proficisci, *set out*
progredi, *to advance*
pugna/proelium, *battle*
pugnare/dimicare, *fight*
redire, *return*
resistere, *resist*
sagitta, *arrow*
scutum, *shield*
se dedere, *surrender*
sequi/persequi, *pursue*

se recipere/pedem referre, *retreat*
servare, *save/keep safe/preserve*
signum, *two distinct meanings, (a) a sign/signal (b) a military standard*
societas, *an alliance*
socius, *an ally*
statio, *outpost/picket/position*
superare/vincere, *conquer/overcome*
tabernaculum, *tent*
telum, *missile*
transfuga, *a deserter*
transfugere, *desert*
transire, *cross*
vulnerare, *wound*
vulnus, -eris, *a wound*

Appendix B

Words easily confused

The possibilities for confusion are enormous. E.g., in the 1972 Examination, I noted several candidates who confused abibo = 'I shall go away' with bibo = 'I drink'. The list below is merely a selection of the commoner specimens.

at, *but*
et, *and*

atque, *and*
itaque, *thereforeland so*

aetas, *age*
aestas, *summer*
aestus, *heatltide*

ager, *field*
agger, *rampart*

audire, *hear*
audere, *dare*

alter, *one or other (of two)*
autem, *butlmoreover*
alius, *otherlanother*

aura, *breeze*
auris, *ear*
aurum, *gold*

cadere, *fall*
caedere, *kill*

cohors, *cohort*
cohortari, *encourage*

consistere, constiti, *haltltake up position*
constituere, constitui, *decideldetermine*

eo, *there (to that place)*
eo, *abl. of* **is, ea, id**

facies, *facelappearance*
facile, *easily*

fama, *famelreputation*
fames, *hungerlfamine*

fere, *almost*
ferre, *carrylbring*

ferrum, *iron*
ferus, *fierce*
fera, *wild animal*

forte, *by chance*
fortiter, *bravely*

fugare, *put to flight*
fugere, *flee*

gens, *racelfamily*
genus –eris, *kindltype*
genu, *knee*

inter, *amonglbetween*
intra, *within*

iter itineris, *journeylmarch*
iterum, *againla second time*

iam, *nowlalready*
nam, *for*

latus, *broadlwide*
latus –eris, *sidelflank*

lex legis, *law*
legere, *chooselread*
levis, *light (in weight)*

liber, *book*
liber, *free*
liberi, *children*

mens, *mind*
mensis, *month*

miles, *soldier*
mille, *thousand*

mos moris, *habitlcustom*
mox, *soon*
mora, *a delay*
mors, *death*
morari, *delay*

mori, *die*

os oris, *mouth*
ora, *shore*

parare, *prepare*
parere, *obey*
parcere, *spare*

porta, *door/gate*
portus, *harbour*

posse, *be able*
potiri, *get possession of*

prodere, *betray*
prodesse, *to benefit*

quaerere, *seek*
queri, *complain*

quidem, *indeed*
ne . . .quidem, *not even*
quidam, quaedam, quoddam,
a certain (person or thing)

quisque, *each*
quoque, *also*

redire, *return (go back)*

reddere, *return (give back)*

sol, *sun*
solum, *soil*
solus, *alone*
solere, *be accustomed*

somnus, *sleep*
somnium, *dream*

statim, *at once/immediately*
simul, *at the same time*

superare, *conquer/overcome*
superesse, *survive*

valles -is, *valley*
vallum, *rampart*

vincere, *conquer/overcome*
vincire, *bind*

vitare, *avoid*
vivere, *live*

via, *road*
vis, *force*
vix, *scarcely*
vita, *life*